D1298533

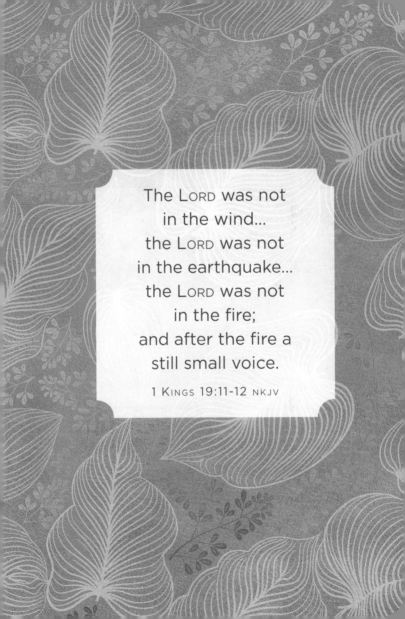

The Lord was not
in the wind...
the Lord was not
in the earthquake...
the Lord was not
in the fire;
and after the fire a
still small voice.

1 Kings 19:11-12 NKJV

INTRODUCTION

How do you hear God's voice? Very few of us experience him speaking audibly. More often we hear him in the quiet. In the stillness. In the moments we are searching for answers and taking the time to listen. He also speaks to us through his Word.

This devotional takes you through the words of Jesus, spoken when he walked the earth. As you quiet yourself and meditate on these Scriptures, devotions, and prayers, you will discover the many facets of his character.

Experience his goodness, faithfulness, compassion, and perfect peace. Spend each day listening for his still small voice. Let him guide you with his wisdom, encourage you with his love, and fill you with confidence as he speaks purpose over your life.

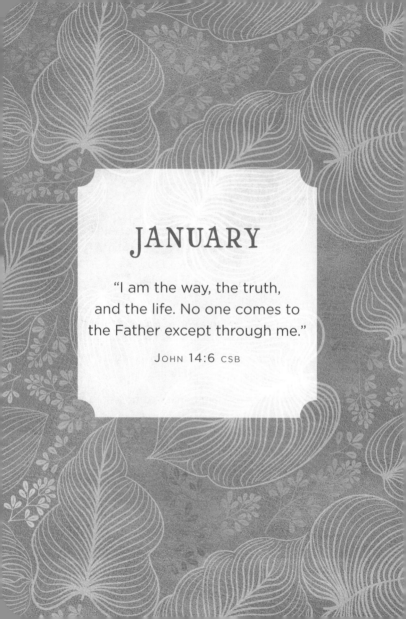

JANUARY

"I am the way, the truth,
and the life. No one comes to
the Father except through me."

JOHN 14:6 CSB

PERSONAL INVITATION

"Come, follow me."
JOHN 1:43 NLT

Just as Jesus invited his disciples, so he says to you, "Come, follow me." Have you taken him up on his offer? Have you left your comfort zone and old way of doing things? Have you let yourself be drawn to his wonders and kindness?

Following Jesus transforms your life. When you take in his wisdom and let his perspective challenge your preconceived notions, your old way of thinking will feel inadequate. There is much to discover in the journey of knowing him. Will you receive his kindness and move toward him? Though the details of your future are unknown, the character of Christ will never change as you travel with him as your friend, healer, teacher, and savior. There is both mystery and hope; there is peace and expectation. Your heart's curiosity can lead you closer to the one who calls you.

Lord Jesus, I choose to follow you not knowing what that will look like in every circumstance or season. I trust your character. I want to know you more.

GENTLE STRENGTH

"What blessing comes to you when gentleness
lives in you! For you will inherit the earth."
MATTHEW 5:5 TPT

When we live with gentleness and humility, we leave room
to grow in understanding and love. When we approach life
with compassion, we make room to change our minds, alter
course, and ask for forgiveness when we miss the mark.

Psalm 37:11 says, "The humble of heart will inherit every
promise and enjoy abundant peace." When you remain
moldable and open to the teaching of Christ, your life is
transformed as you yield to and partner with his ways.
Psalm 149:4 says, "For he enjoys his faithful lovers. He
adorns the humble with his beauty, and he loves to
give them victory." In Christ's victory, you find your own.
Abandon pursuits that lead you away from his love and
pattern your life after Jesus who adorns you with his
beautiful mercy.

Christ Jesus, I don't want to protect my selfish
tendencies, and I don't want to wander away from your
love. May love be a banner over my life in all I do, say,
and how I treat others.

EVERY LITTLE THING

"Even the very hairs of your head are all numbered."
MATTHEW 10:30 NIV

God knows not only our names and ages but every detail about us. He cares deeply about the smallest aspects of life. Jesus illustrated this by saying he knows the number of hairs on our heads. It's such a specific, nearly impossible thing to know, yet he takes notice of things that seem absurd to us. There are no limits to his understanding.

Why worry with a detailed and loving God overlooking our lives? Let's put our wholehearted trust in him and turn over our anxieties to his patient presence. He is enough to sustain us, and he will provide what we need. Every little thing is covered by him.

Lord Jesus, thank you for the revelation of the Father's detailed attention and care for his children. I trust you with what I can't control or anticipate. Nothing surprises you; I can rest in you today.

TIMING MATTERS

"The time is fulfilled, and the kingdom of God is at hand; repent and believe in the gospel."

MARK 1:15 NASB

Today's verse is the theme of Jesus' ministry. He didn't wait to share the news. Whom Jesus taught, his confidence in his identity, and the welcoming compassion he offered to those that society dismissed was both beautiful and radical.

Jesus fulfilled prophecies that had buoyed the hopes of the Jewish people for centuries. He was their promised Messiah, but he is also the Savior for everyone who believes. Have you experienced the kingdom of Christ in your life? Have you turned your life back to God and put your trust in his good news? Here is an invitation to turn to him and experience his fullness. Today is the day of salvation!

Jesus Christ, I believe you are the way, the truth, and the life. I want to know the power of your love not only in my heart but in my life. I come to you with an open heart ready to receive from the abundance you offer.

TRUSTWORTHY

"Whoever can be trusted with a little can also be trusted with a lot, and whoever is dishonest with a little is dishonest with a lot."

LUKE 16:10 NCV

Jesus is talking about money here, but the principle applies to all areas of life. When we have resources that could benefit others instead of us, it takes integrity, self-discipline, and honor to do the right thing. Honesty paired with reliability is powerful. Whoever can be trusted with a little will earn trust with more.

Think of Joseph from the Old Testament. He was sold into slavery by his brothers, and everything was taken from him. However, that was only the beginning of his story. He was as trustworthy as they come. Proving himself a hard, reliable, and honest worker, he rose through the ranks to become trusted advisor to the king. He started with nothing, but he ended up being one of the most powerful men in Egypt.

Jesus, I want to live with integrity before your eyes and before others. It doesn't matter how little or how much I have; I want to honor you and those who trust me. Teach me, Lord, to always choose the trustworthy and righteous way.

SENT IN PEACE

Jesus said to them again, "Peace to you!
As the Father has sent Me, I also send you."
JOHN 20:21 NKJV

After the long, dark days of his crucifixion and burial,
Jesus reappeared to his disciples. He encouraged
them and commissioned them the way the Father had
commissioned him. He gave them the authority to preach
forgiveness of sins in the power of his name.

What he did for them, he does for us. He comes in peace,
and he sends us out in the peace of his Spirit. What Christ
experienced, he offers to share with us. He offers us the
resurrection power that he walks in as well. We only yield
to his leadership and remain obedient to his law of love.
As we do, we will reflect his likeness to those around us.

Jesus, give me the peace of your presence. You are the
one I follow, and I trust you to move in power through
my surrendered life. May your grace, love, and peace
overflow my life as I am continually filled and led by you.

NO DETAIL OVERLOOKED

Jesus answered him, "Allow it for now,
because this is the way for us to fulfill all righteousness."
Then John allowed him to be baptized.
MATTHEW 3:15 CSB

Jesus sought out John the Baptist knowing that he needed to be baptized by him. This was before the start of his ministry. John resisted and questioned why he should baptize Jesus when he felt as if Jesus should baptize him. John wasn't being falsely humble; he knew Jesus was anointed by God the Father.

Jesus pointed out that the fulfillment of the law was required, and this was part of it. Every prophecy needed to be satisfied. God didn't overlook a single detail, and even though John did not recognize what was happening at the time, Jesus already saw. We can trust Jesus' timing, wisdom, and offerings because he knows what we can't comprehend.

Son of God, you are worthy of my trust. Thank you for being patient with me even when I question what you are doing. I look to you now.

FORGIVENESS

When Jesus saw their faith, he said to the paralyzed man,
"Son, your sins are forgiven."
MARK 2:5 NIV

Before Jesus healed the paralyzed man, he did something even more powerful; he removed his guilt, shame, and fear. On behalf of the Father, he forgave the man's sins. The Pharisees balked at this. They wanted to know what authority gave Jesus the right to do such a thing. In Jewish law, cleansing sacrifices needed to be offered in strict ways by specific people. Jesus broke the mold by releasing the man from guilt. Why and how did he do this? Because he is the Son of God, and he came to set captives free.

What God does not hold against us, may we refuse to hold against each other or ourselves. May we liberate others with our forgiveness. Only God can remove our guilt, and Jesus Christ has already done that. We can trust him and let his mercy empower our acts of forgiveness. What we let go of, we can leave to the Lord.

Savior, thank you for your forgiveness. Thank you for setting me free from the guilt and shame that comes with imperfection. I am alive and free in your mercy.

TRUST HIM

When he had finished speaking, he said to Simon,
"Now go out where it is deeper,
and let down your nets to catch some fish."
LUKE 5:4 NLT

In return for letting him use his boat as a place to teach the crowds from, Jesus gave Simon Peter a gift. Though Simon had just returned from fishing all night without any luck, Jesus told him to row out into deeper water and cast his nets. Simon was skeptical, but he did as Jesus instructed.

When Simon pulled up the nets, they were ready to burst from the load of fish they held! Simon Peter's response was remarkably humble. Knowing the state of his heart and life, he told Jesus to leave him. He did not feel worthy of Jesus' attention. Even so, we know that Jesus would eventually build his church on the rock of Peter. He was one of the forefathers of Christianity. Don't count yourself out when Jesus wants to teach you to walk in the power of his ways.

Lord Jesus, I know how good you are and how I fail to meet your standards, and I am astounded by your love. I will follow you and let your kindness draw me in. I surrender to your leadership; there's no one better than you.

WAIT ON HIM

Jesus instructed them, "Don't leave Jerusalem,
but wait here until you receive the gift I told you about,
the gift the Father has promised."
ACTS 1:4 TPT

Sometimes we need to move ahead in life. Other times, waiting is necessary. Why would we rush ahead in our own strength when God offers us the strength of his Spirit to empower us? When he tells you to wait, listen. There is purpose in all he does.

The Holy Spirit is a generous gift. Fellowship with the Spirit infuses our inner beings with peace, love, joy, endurance, and hope. The fruit of the Spirit can be witnessed in the lives of those submitted to him. The Holy Spirit transforms us from the inside out and gives us all we need to experience the fullness of God's life within us. Take time to wait on the Lord each day and ask the Holy Spirit to fill you with what you need to thrive in every circumstance and challenge.

Lord, knowing you is the deep work of your Spirit within me. I wait on you today; fill me with the powerful love of your Spirit.

RELEASE YOUR WORRIES

"Let not your hearts be troubled.
Believe in God; believe also in me."
JOHN 14:1 ESV

We can't escape the troubles of the world, but we can keep our hearts tethered to the one who does the heavy lifting of our burdens. Jesus is marvelous in mercy; he is generous in grace and compassion. He offers us the shelter of a faithful friend. He extends the same safety that a reliable parent does to their child.

What is troubling your heart today? Instead of surrendering to fear, can you surrender it to the Lord? Jesus Christ is capable of carrying all your concerns, and he will not forget to provide for your needs. Will you trust him? Will you take him at his Word and allow his peace to permeate your heart? He is close. Lean in and let go.

Jesus, I don't want to carry the weight of these worries or be afraid that if I misplace one, I will somehow suffer for it. I am suffering under the weight of them. I offer you my fear, anxiety, and concerns, and I receive your rest, peace, and help. I believe in you.

FREE TO GROW

"Others are like the seed planted among the thorny weeds. They hear the teaching, but the worries of this life, the temptation of wealth, and many other evil desires keep the teaching from growing and producing fruit in their lives."

MARK 4:18-19 NCV

Is something stunting your spiritual growth? What keeps you from developing in faith? What thoughts, desires, or fears entangle your mind and heart? We are human, and we all fall short of the glory of God. Fortunately, it doesn't matter how long you have followed the Lord; he always offers more grace when you turn to him.

Think of things that deplete your hope and belief. Conversely, what are the things that (and the people who) infuse you with peace and hope? Whatever is leeching the life out of you, offer it to the Lord. Whatever fills you with the liberating love and life of the Lord, give it more of your attention. When you are free from thorny weeds, you will produce powerful fruit from the Spirit's life within you.

Christ Jesus, I want my life to produce your abundant fruit. Where I am holding on to limiting beliefs, disentangle me with your liberating love and powerful wisdom. I am yours.

UNNECESSARY WEIGHT

"Take nothing for the road," he told them,
"no staff, no traveling bag, no bread, no money;
and don't take an extra shirt."
LUKE 9:3 CSB

As Jesus was commissioning his apostles to go on what would be their first ministry trip, he gave them very specific instructions. No staff or bread? No money? Jesus knew they already had what they needed. God does not always ask us to not prepare ourselves, but he always wants us to rely on his powerful mercy.

Have you ever felt like God was leading you to do something risky? We can't know all the reasons behind Jesus' instructions that the disciples take anything extra on their journey, but we do know they were relying strictly on the provision and power of God. Will you trust Jesus to do the same for you when he asks you to leave your comfort behind?

Lord Jesus, I don't want to have excuses for why I shouldn't rely on your help. I want your power to move through my life. Give me greater faith to trust you will go with me no matter where I go. Give me courage to take risks while on your path.

LET IT GO

"Whenever you stand praying, if you have anything against anyone, forgive him, that your Father in heaven may also forgive you your trespasses."
MARK 11:25 NKJV

When our hearts remain full of offense toward another, it can keep us from the fullness of God's love. We love because he first loved us; this is what the Scriptures teach. With God's love as our foundation and unlimited supply, the more we give, the more we can receive. God has fully forgiven us in Christ, so why would we withhold our forgiveness from others?

Unforgiveness grows like a bitter, choking root in our hearts; choosing to forgive frees us. Even when we are justified in our anger and offense, Jesus is our healer, but he can only mend what we let him near. Will we soften our hearts, choose to extend grace, and let Jesus meet the needs that others have overlooked? We need not allow the mistakes of others to limit our growth.

Jesus, you are the only one perfect in love. You do not withhold your affection, and you don't manipulate your mercy. I want to be like you. Help me forgive those who have hurt me and let go of the possibility of it being any other way. I choose your mercy.

STUMBLING BLOCK

When Jesus heard this, he said, "Healthy people don't need a doctor—sick people do." Then he added, "Now go and learn the meaning of this Scripture: 'I want you to show mercy, not offer sacrifices.' For I have come to call not those who think they are righteous, but those who know they are sinners."

MATTHEW 9:12-13 NLT

The religious elite of Jesus' day judged Jesus and those he chose to spend time with. Did this change how Jesus acted? No. He was never in the wrong. He still ministered to the sick, the poor, and the outcast. He spoke up for women and turned the tables on those who claimed to know what God was about and yet used their influence to line their pockets.

Are we letting pride stand in the way of understanding Jesus and what he is about? He puts no limits on the love of the Father. Do we? Do we keep ourselves from treating others with kindness because we think our contempt is excusable? Instead of letting pride keep us from leading with love, we can follow the example of Jesus who broke down barriers instead of maintaining them.

Jesus, I humble myself in your love. I don't want pride to keep me from living out the fullness of your generous mercy. Cut away my pride today.

NOTHING TO HIDE

"Be on your guard against the yeast of the Pharisees, which is hypocrisy. There is nothing concealed that will not be disclosed, or hidden that will not be made known."

LUKE 12:1-2 NIV

Hypocrisy means requiring a certain standard while living by a different measure. It means claiming to value one thing while not following through with actions to support it. Pride can lead us to hypocrisy if we're not careful. It affords grace to us while limiting it for others, and this is not the way of Jesus.

God knows our hearts. He judges not just what others see but the true intentions of a person. When we yield our hearts to Christ, his mercy washes us. He removes the stain of our guilt. Then, we get to extend that gracious compassion to others. May we live as true, honest, and honorable followers of Christ with nothing to hide.

Jesus Christ, your love requires my submission to work through my life. I don't want to withhold anything from you; I don't know better than you do. Help me live as trustworthy, reliable, and completely surrendered to you.

EVERYTHING CLEAR

"Whatever you have said in the dark shall be heard in the light, and what you have whispered in private rooms shall be proclaimed on the housetops."

LUKE 12:3 ESV

We can't hide anything from God. If we, behind closed doors, whisper secrets we would never want exposed in public, we may want to reevaluate our hearts and let the Lord's light of conviction shine on us. With humility, we can start afresh. With the mercy of Christ, we are empowered to change.

If there is anything in your life that doesn't align with the values of Christ's kingdom, take this opportunity to allow him to shape your mindset in his love. It might be simple prayer: "I know I don't know everything. I know I don't have everything right, Lord. Teach me your ways." That is a prayer of humility. Begin there and allow the love of Christ to transform your heart, mind, and life in his mercy.

Lord, I don't want to live with a false sense of certainty about my abilities or rights. You are King of my life, and I surrender to you and your ways. Shape me and transform me in your love so I may be a shining beacon of your glorious promise to all who know me.

THE FATHER'S WORK

"I speak to you timeless truth. The Son is not able to do anything from himself or through my own initiative. I only do the works that I see the Father doing, for the Son does the same works as his Father."

JOHN 5:19 TPT

Today's verse holds a powerful statement from Jesus; he said he did nothing on his own initiative. Every person he healed, every merciful act he performed, every prayer he prayed, he did to represent the heart and will of the Father.

If you are familiar with the goodness of Christ, you are familiar with the goodness of the Father. The earth is full of the glory of the Lord, and Jesus reminded people of this. The glory of God, more powerful than we can imagine, is also indescribably beautiful. What causes wonder to rise in our hearts or hope to take root? As we look at the ministry of Jesus, as we soak in the wonders of his recorded Word, may awe lead us into deeper fellowship with Spirit, Son, and Father. They are one, and they are accessible even now.

Loving Lord, I can't begin to describe the wonder in my heart when I consider your goodness. I want to know you in deeper ways. Reveal more of your incredible nature as I turn to you today.

HIDDEN TREASURE

"The kingdom of heaven is like a treasure hidden in a field. One day a man found the treasure, and then he hid it in the field again. He was so happy that he went and sold everything he owned to buy that field."

MATTHEW 13:44 NCV

Imagine finding a secret treasure no one else had uncovered. What would you do? Would you take it all, leave some behind, or look for the rights to it? The kingdom of God is more glorious, fulfilling, and promising than golden treasure. When we find it, we are encouraged to give all we have to gain the rights to it.

When we surrender ourselves to Christ, we let go of what no longer serves us and receive what he offers. What he offers is far better than anything we leave behind. Do you trust that Jesus is as good as the Word of God says? Spend time in his presence today and ask him to reveal the glorious treasure of his kingdom. Seek and you will find.

Wonderful Jesus, I give all I have to belong to your kingdom. I don't want to experience the abundance of your kingdom only when you return and restore the earth; I want it here in the nitty-gritty of this life.

POWER OF PEACE

He got up and rebuked the wind and said to the sea,
"Hush, be still." And the wind died down
and it became perfectly calm.

MARK 4:39 NASB

Jesus had the power to calm raging seas when he walked this earth, and he still has that power today. He does not defeat storms by raging louder than they do; he speaks peace to the wind and waves, and they calm in response. Instead of relying on shows of brute force to face the storms of life, we can follow Jesus' lead and release peace.

What comes to mind when you think of peacekeepers? Do you imagine them weak? Or do you recognize the power of meeting chaos, trouble, and pressure without threats of violence? This isn't the only time Jesus displayed peace in chaos. When the guards came to take him away in the garden of Gethsemane, his disciples drew their weapons and fought. Jesus told them to put their swords away. Are we brave enough to follow his lead?

Jesus Christ, your ways are so different from mine. I find this again and again, and it challenges me to my core. Please fill my heart with your peace and give me courage to use it.

WHAT YOU CAN HANDLE

"I still have many things to tell you,
but you can't bear them now."
JOHN 16:12 CSB

God does not give us all the information we will need at once. It would be too much for us to handle. He does, however, give us wisdom and direction for each step. Do we trust that even though we can't see the future, he is with us and will to guide us?

Pursuing the Lord for answers is a wonderful and valuable quest. As we get to know God's character more, especially his faithfulness as he walks with us through the hills and the valleys of this life, we learn to trust that what he offers is enough for the present moment. There is more than enough grace. There is love that overwhelmingly sustains us. He gives us what we need, so let's not get ahead of ourselves worrying about the future.

Lord, slow me down when I need all the answers. Keep me grounded in your love which pulls me back to the present and directs my attention to your gracious provision and wisdom here and now.

NEW VESSELS

"Who pours new wine into an old wineskin? If someone did, the old wineskin would burst and the new wine would be lost. New wine must always be poured into new wineskins."
LUKE 5:37-38 TPT

When new things are birthed in your life, you can outgrow the bounds of what once felt comfortable and safe. Why try to fit your new body into clothes that no longer fit? Why use the same habits to replicate a different goal? When there is significant change, take it as an opportunity to evaluate what no longer serves you in this coming season no matter how good it was for you in the past.

God has made us new creations in Christ. We are not just repaired but completely new. We need not act as we did before and only serve our personal needs and interests. Let's allow the merciful mind of Christ to transform our thinking. His guidance will lead us into new territory where new tools are needed. Behold, he is doing a new thing. Do you not perceive it?

Lord Jesus, I don't want to stay stuck in old habits or ways of doing things just because it is what I have known. I want to trust you more than my own understanding. Please help me grow.

TRANSFORMATION

Jesus did not let him, but said, "Go home to your own people and tell them how much the Lord has done for you, and how he has had mercy on you."

MARK 5:19 NIV

It is important we know what Jesus is saying to us as individuals. While Jesus beckoned some to follow him, when this man he had healed asked to become a disciple, Jesus sent him home. Was his assignment any less important? No. He had a powerful testimony of God's goodness to share with those who knew him well.

Are you longing to do what others are doing but feel you have lost your sense of self? Look to Jesus. He has specific assignments that are for you and no one else. Seek his wisdom and yield your life to his guidance. God's mercy is at work in your life in tangible ways, and sometimes that is exactly you are to share with others.

Jesus, thank you for the reminder that my life and calling are unique. Speak to me with your Spirit and show me the way to go. You have been good to me, and I trust you will continue to be.

WORDS TO SHARE

"Have no fear of them, for nothing is covered that will not be revealed, or hidden that will not be known. What I tell you in the dark, say in the light, and what you hear whispered, proclaim on the housetops."

MATTHEW 10:26-27 ESV

When others threaten us, Jesus tells us not to fear them. Does that sound unrealistic? The presence of God is with us, and even when others look for ways to tear us down, he sees every motivation that is hidden from our view. Everything will be revealed at the right time. As we wait, we can put our hope in Christ and do as he says.

What God shares with us can be shared with others. He doesn't want us to keep it to ourselves. This is why he says, "What I tell you in the dark, say in the light." We will know the right time to share what he has told us. May we have the wisdom to speak when he urges us to and remain silent when the timing is not right. We have nothing to fear when our hearts and motivations are pure before God.

Righteous One, speak to my heart today and deepen my understanding of your kingdom. I want to know what you want me to share. I am listening.

HEALING FAITH

Jesus said, "Someone deliberately touched me,
for I felt healing power go out from me."
"Daughter," he said to her, "your faith
has made you well. Go in peace."
Luke 8:46, 48 nlt

When determination and faith drive us, no one can keep
us from what we set our hearts and minds upon. For the
woman in today's Scripture, her faith in Christ as healer led
her to get close enough to touch the hem of Jesus' robe.
As soon as she touched it, she was healed.

Jesus felt the power go out from him. Was he upset about
it? No, but he wanted that person to step forward. When
the woman realized she could not hide, she fell at Jesus'
feet and trembled She told him that she knew if she
touched the edge of his garment, she believed she would
be healed. And she was! Jesus commended her faith and
sent her forth free from shame.

**Jesus, you are my healer and my liberator. Remove the
shame I carry and heal wounds that need your powerful
touch. I want to have faith like this courageous woman.**

PROPER PERSPECTIVE

Jesus said, "If you were blind, you would not be guilty of sin. But since you keep saying you see, your guilt remains."
JOHN 9:41 NCV

When we are young, we can't grasp the understanding adults have. In the same way, when we are innocent in our limited perspectives, we can only do better when we know better. With maturity, we see through hindsight what we didn't know at the time. It teaches us to loosen our grasp on what we feel is certain right now; it may change with further time, experience, and perspective.

God will not despise a humble heart. Why? Because it is teachable. It can admit when and where it is wrong, seek forgiveness and restoration, and make necessary changes with new information. We must keep estimations of ourselves grounded in the reality that we are still learning. Then, Jesus can direct our yielded hearts in his love and truth.

Jesus, I humble myself before you today. Thank you for receiving me whenever I come to you. Forgive me for times I have misunderstood your ways and used them as a weapon against others. May your love right the wrong perspectives I have.

DILIGENT CURIOSITY

"Take care what you listen to.
By your standard of measure it will be measured to you;
and more will be given you besides."
MARK 4:24 NASB

How diligent are we to understand what we hear? Do we take in information without questioning its validity or source? There is wisdom in letting curiosity lead us. Depending on how much we want to understand, that is the measure that will satisfy us. If we don't care to know what's under the surface, we won't do the work of due diligence.

Do we bristle at questions others pose about our beliefs? Perhaps this points to a lack of freedom with our curiosity. God welcomes our questions. Those who truly are trying to understand are met with the mercy of Christ. Throw aside any notions of faith refusing to engage in healthy conversation and let curiosity awaken in your heart.

Jesus, I want to grapple with questions that make others uncomfortable. I want to truly understand, and to do that, I have to learn to listen and not jump in with an answer. Keep my heart and mind open.

UNENCUMBERED FAITH

"Leave the little children alone, and don't try to keep them from coming to me, because the kingdom of heaven belongs to such as these."

MATTHEW 19:14 CSB

A child's innocent view on life is pure and uniquely wonderful. Where adults often overthink, children simply act. In today's verse, the children ran to Jesus because they were drawn to him. They didn't overthink it or talk themselves out of coming to him. They followed their instinct.

May we come to Jesus with the same heart of absolute faith and not let worry, fear, or skepticism keep us away. He welcomes us with open arms. We can run into his presence with expectation, and he embraces us with his wonderful affection when we do. He is delighted by our presence and pursuit, so let's throw off our worries about how we appear and come to him.

Jesus, you are always ready to receive those who come to you. I don't hesitate today to turn toward you. Flood me with the loving light of your presence as I do. I love you!

WITHIN AND WITHOUT

"Hear Me, everyone, and understand: There is nothing that enters a man from outside which can defile him; but the things which come out of him, those are the things that defile a man. If anyone has ears to hear, let him hear!"

MARK 7:14-16 NKJV

In Jewish tradition, there is a lot said about what one should and shouldn't eat. In the Old Testament, some of the many directives given to the Israelites included foods to avoid. It is no wonder, then, that the religious leaders of Jesus' day thought a person could be defiled by unclean foods.

When our given guidelines become more important than our relationships and compassion, we have lost sight of the true purpose of the law. This is what Jesus was getting at. We are not to judge others on the surface things they do or don't do. Instead, we focus on our hearts, how we act toward others, and the attitudes we cultivate.

Jesus Christ, thank you for setting the record straight and pointing us to the heart of the Father. I want to walk in your love and not in judgment of my neighbor. Align me with your values and teach me to lead with compassion.

CHOOSE WISELY

"Remember this: everyone with a lofty opinion of who he is and who seeks to raise himself up will be humbled before all. And everyone with a modest opinion of who he is and chooses to humble himself will be raised up before all."

LUKE 14:11 TPT

When we strive for approval in the eyes of others by overselling what we can offer, failure is inevitable. Pride pushes us to appear as something we are not, but humility is softer and more real. It allows for the grace to change and to make things right when we are wrong. It leaves room for growth unlike the false confidence of pride.

We can walk the humble path. We can do the work that is ours to do and not act like anything is below us. No matter what our status, we can remain humble and hardworking. We mustn't let the deceit of pride keep us from the grace of God we desperately need.

Lord, I am no better than anyone else. May I resist pride that judges others against my ideals rather than their worth in you. Your way is better.

ROOM FOR MORE

Jesus answered her, "If you knew the gift of God, and who it is that is saying to you, 'Give me a drink,' you would have asked him, and he would have given you living water."
JOHN 4:10 ESV

When we go to Jesus with what we need, he delivers. There is nothing too small or too big to ask the Lord. He is our help in every need, so don't limit the power of God's love in your life by assuming you have reached its limit.

Approach today with eyes that see Jesus with you. Keep his presence near your thoughts as you go about your day. Just as you would carry on a conversation with a friend, keep an open line of communication. There is always more grace, strength, joy, peace, love, and power in his presence. Drink from his well of living water and be satisfied.

Provider, my soul thirsts for you. I long to be aware of your presence in the details of my life. May I hear your voice when you speak, and may I not hold back a single thought or question from you today. Fill me up, Lord.

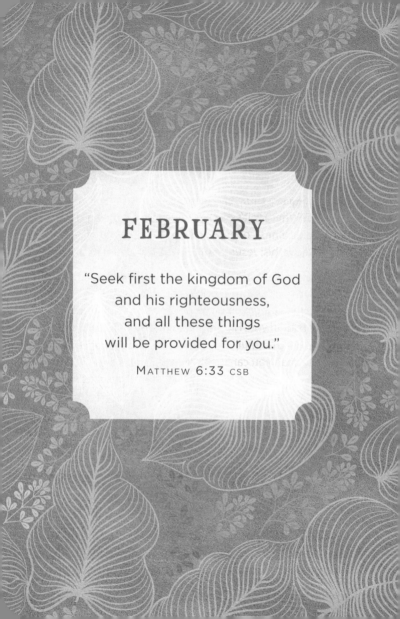

FEBRUARY

"Seek first the kingdom of God
and his righteousness,
and all these things
will be provided for you."

MATTHEW 6:33 CSB

WILLING ONE

Jesus reached out his hand and touched the man.
"I am willing," he said. "Be clean!"
And immediately the leprosy left him.
LUKE 5:13 NIV

Are you dealing with something that saps all your strength? Whether it's the loss of a loved one, the struggle of a chronic illness, or an issue that keeps you feeling lonely, know this: Jesus is willing to take the weight of your burden and heal you.

More than anything, may you know the comfort of his presence, the tangible goodness of his love, and the peace of his delight in you. He cares for you not in theory but in practice. He is faithful, and he will not ignore you. He loves you more than you can imagine, and he speaks words of life over you. Listen for his voice which brings relief, comfort, joy, and peace.

Healer, I ask for your help. Bring relief to the parts of me that are tired, worn down, and in desperate need of your touch. Revive me in your mercy today.

SMALL BEGINNINGS

"How can I describe the Kingdom of God? What story
should I use to illustrate it? It is like a mustard seed
planted in the ground. It is the smallest of all seeds, but
it becomes the largest of all garden plants; it grows long
branches, and birds can make nests in its shade."
MARK 4:30-32 NLT

No matter how small your belief starts out, it can grow
bigger and bigger until it flourishes into a resting place for
others. A seed is not sown to become a sturdy plant the
next day. It takes time, attention, and nourishment to grow.

Look to the light of the Lord and soak up the nourishment
of his presence. Send your roots deep into the soil of his
love. Let his truth direct your trajectory. He is the divine
gardener, and you are under his care. He will prune you
with his wisdom, and his kindness will cultivate trust to
grow in the direction he leads you. No matter where you
are today in this journey, you are unfolding new leaves
under his care.

Jesus, I trust your attention to detail and your wisdom
to guide, prune, and love me to life in your tender care.
I am yours, and I won't stop trusting you.

QUIET GIVING

"When you give to the poor, don't be like the hypocrites. They blow trumpets in the synagogues and on the streets so that people will see them and honor them. I tell you the truth, those hypocrites already have their full reward."

MATTHEW 6:2 NCV

Generosity is one of the core values of God's kingdom. If we want to be like Jesus, we can't ignore the importance of giving to others. There is always a return on gifts we give, but Jesus reminds us to wait on God for our true reward. Out of a heart of love, we can give to the Lord and others and not for praise from those who know what we are doing.

In fact, Jesus takes it even a step further when he says, "when you give to the poor, don't let anyone know what you are doing" (Matthew 6:3). When you give to the poor, Jesus says, not if. Do we make giving to the poor a priority by building it into our budgets? If not, now is the time to set it up. Do it quietly unto the Lord; it is an act of worship and stewardship.

Jesus, I want to be more generous with my resources and to give with a heart of love. I do not seek to gain favor with others. Help me follow your ways.

CONFIDENT FAITH

"I have told you this so that you would not surrender
to confusion or doubt."

JOHN 16:1 TPT

The "this" Jesus speaks of here can be summed up in what
he said in the previous chapter: "Just remember, when the
unbelieving world hates you, they first hated me" (John
15:18). When we stand on the truth of Christ's love, we
should not be surprised when many people don't like
it. Real love will cost us our pride. It's necessary to stay
humble and close to the Lord to follow his wise example.

The confidence of our faith is not found in how
comfortable or easy our lives are; we all suffer to some
degree. Jesus is the way, the truth, the life, and we come
to the Father freely through him. He is our confidence, and
what he promises is better than anything we can build
in our own strength. When backlash comes, we can lean
further into the grace of his Spirit.

Jesus, may my roots go deep into the truth of who you
are and not in the comfort or ease of my circumstances.
You are better, your ways truer, and your love more
gracious then the world could ever be.

TRUST THE TIMING

"It is not for you to know times or periods
that the Father has set by his own authority."
ACTS 1:7 CSB

Just as Jesus told his disciples that it was not their
responsibility to know the timing of his coming kingdom,
we can't guess either. We can recognize the seasons we
are in and act accordingly, but no one can know the exact
timing of the Lord's fulfillment of his promises. We can
trust him anyway, for he is faithful to do all he said he
would do.

It's easier to trust a reliable friend than to trust a stranger
whose character is unknown to us. How well do we know
the Lord? How close are we to him? The good news is we
always have room to grow, and every moment is a fresh
opportunity to turn toward him. Instead of looking ahead
to try to control our expectations of the future, we can
look to the character of our Savior and build a stronger
relationship with him.

Lord, it is easier to trust you when I remember your
goodness, faithfulness, and merciful kindness. May
my heart be more satisfied in knowing you rather than
making a guessing game of the future.

UNDERSTANDABLE TERMS

Then He said to them, "Follow Me,
and I will make you fishers of men."
MATTHEW 4:19 NKJV

Jesus met each of his disciples where they were, and he called them in ways that built on their experience. Simon Peter, Andrew, Jacob, and John were all fishermen. Jesus called them to follow him and fish for men. Though it may sound funny to our ears, it must have been a captivating offer for these men to leave their livelihoods behind to follow him.

Just as Jesus spoke their language, he speaks yours. He knows the language of your heart and the experience and skills you have, and he calls you to follow him. Have you experienced the Lord enlightening and drawing your heart to him by speaking to you personally? His Spirit is with you to open your ears, bring understanding, and draw you closer to him as he teaches you the ways of his kingdom.

Lord Jesus, I know you say, "Call to me and I will answer," but I offer the same to you. My heart is open. Speak, and I will listen. Call, and I will answer. I am yours.

DOING GOOD

He said to them, "Is it lawful to do good on the Sabbath or
to do harm, to save a life or to kill?" But they kept silent.
MARK 3:4 NASB

What does it mean to do good? Is it not found in actions
that produce the fruit of the Spirit? As Galatians 3 says,
it is "love, joy, peace, patience, kindness, goodness,
faithfulness, gentleness, self-control; against such things
there is no law" (vs. 22–23). There is no law against these
things because there doesn't need to be.

When we live with the fruit of the Spirit as our guiding
values in relationships, work, and all interactions, we
have nothing to fear. Doing good is letting love lead us,
allowing the pursuit of peace to be better than being
right, and showing kindness rather than biting back. Let
us freely follow the directives of Jesus and do good no
matter what day it is.

Faithful One, following your wisdom will lead me further
into doing good rather than away from it. Help me
choose to do what you did even when it makes others
uncomfortable.

CIVIC RESPONSIBILITY

"Then render to Caesar the things that are Caesar's,
and to God the things that are God's."
LUKE 20:25 ESV

Our responsibilities in life are not only to God; they are
to the people around us as well. We can't claim to love
God, yet rebel against the laws of the land because we
don't agree with them. We give to the government what is
theirs, and we give to God what is his.

Sometimes, we complicate what it means to live with
integrity. Do we love God with our hearts and actions?
Do we love others without prejudice, manipulation, or
conditions? Do we obey local laws? Do we follow through
on what we say we will do? Do we honor others the way
we want to be honored? We fulfill our responsibilities by
living openly, honestly, with nothing to hide, and with no
reason to hurl insults toward anyone.

Lord Jesus, I have a lot of growing to do in your love.
Where I want to withhold, you encourage growing in
generosity. I don't want to avoid my responsibilities,
either. I want to embrace them. May my life honor you.

NOTHING WASTED

When they had all had enough to eat, he said to his
disciples, "Gather the pieces that are left over.
Let nothing be wasted."
JOHN 6:12 NIV

Nothing, not even leftover bread, is wasted in the
kingdom of Christ. He doesn't overlook any detail. We can
trust his leading, submit to his teaching, and be more like
him. Are there areas of our lives where excess is prevalent?
Perhaps we have overlooked resources we could use to
bless others. With the help of Jesus, we see what we can
offer to others. We don't want to be hoarders; neither
should we be careless.

Practice paying attention and following the wisdom of
the Lord. Be attentive and generous with what you have
include what others may only think of as crumbs. Even the
crumbs matter to God.

Jesus, I don't want to carelessly consume things and
leave a mess in my wake. You care about this world,
about your people, and about more than I can imagine.
Teach me to use every crumb.

IMMERSED IN THE SPIRIT

"John baptized you in water, but in a few days from now
you will be baptized in the Holy Spirit!"
ACTS 1:5 TPT

Jesus gave his disciples the promise of the Holy Spirit on
more than one occasion. This time, however, was just a
few days before he would leave them and ascend to the
Father. The Holy Spirit would come soon after with power,
and they would be filled with the presence of God himself.

The promise of the Holy Spirit was not only for Jesus' first
disciples; it is for all who believe in Christ. The gracious
Spirit of God comes to dwell within us when we submit to
Christ. The power of the Spirit is a visceral experience as
physical as being baptized in water. If you have not known
this baptism, ask Jesus to send the Spirit to immerse you
in waves of his powerful love.

Spirit, I long for the power of your presence to wash over
me, fill me up, and flow through me. I am yours. Reveal
yourself to me.

SPIRITUAL NOURISHMENT

*"No! The Scriptures say, 'People do not live by bread alone,
but by every word that comes from the mouth of God.'"*
MATTHEW 4:4 NLT

Jesus reminded the people he taught that Scripture held more than practical guidelines for everyday life; it was a map to lead us back to the heart of God. God's Word is all about our relationship with the one who created us. It was so in the beginning, and it remains true today.

How much is your spiritual life about following a list of rules, and how much of it is tending to the relationship you have with God? He is accessible. His presence is with you. Christ broke down every barrier and opened the door to the Father's favor. Instead of focusing on being perfect, just listen to the Lord today and follow his lead.

Jesus, thank you for reminding me that the foundation of this relationship is to know you and be known by you. I open my heart to you, look to your Scriptures, and lean into your presence to nourish my soul.

RESIST OFFENSE

"A prophet is honored everywhere except in his hometown and with his own people and in his own home."
MARK 6:4 NCV

Keeping the heart open to hope and change is an important element of faith. We may resist the changes we see in others if we have known them well and for a long time. Our set expectations of them can be at odds with the people they are transforming into. This can be hard to overcome, but it's possible.

The people of Jesus' hometown resisted his message because they took offense at his confidence and message. They had watched him grow up. They had reasons why they thought the Messiah would not look so ordinary. Still, they had the same opportunity as other towns to witness the power of God work through him. Offense can cloud our faith, so we must hold on to the tension of natural realities and the mystery of God's mercy at the same time.

Miracle Worker, you are the God who healed diseases, caused blind eyes to see, and led a generation to the Father's heart. I don't want to keep you in a limiting box based on my own experiences or expectations. You are much larger than that.

SAME POWER

"Go and report to John what you have seen and heard:
The blind receive their sight, the lame walk, those with
leprosy are cleansed, the deaf hear, the dead are raised,
and the poor are told the good news."

Luke 7:22 csb

Jesus ministered in the power of God and not just to
show off what he could do. Preaching good news to the
destitute, raising the dead back to life, opening deaf ears,
healing incurable diseases, and more revealed the love of
the Father in practical ways. Even better, this same power
is still working in the world through the Holy Spirit.

May we find our hope, breakthroughs, peace, joy, and love
rooted in the ministry of Christ through fellowship with his
Spirit. There is nothing he can't do, and he longs to reveal
the love of God in powerful ways in our lives. Look to him,
lean on his strength, and testify about his goodness.

Powerful One, thank you for the ministry of your love
through practical acts of compassion. I long to know
you, not only in my heart, soul, and mind, but in my
embodied experience. Reveal yourself as you minister
to and through me.

DELIGHT IN HIM

"Blessed is he who is not offended because of Me."
LUKE 7:23 NKJV

Jesus had just finished telling John the Baptist's messengers the miraculous fruit of his ministry as an answer to John's question about whether he was the Messiah. Such power at work through Jesus could lead others to be skeptical, jealous, or afraid. Jesus' statement that those who remain unoffended by him are blessed is one we should consider today.

Offense builds a wall around our hearts. It prevents connection and isolates us from the one we are offended by. Jesus said those who come to him with the open curiosity of children are the ones who inherit the kingdom of heaven, so we don't have to ignore our questions. We can bring them to him instead of letting them keep us from him. He is kind and patient with us.

Redeemer, I come to you with all my questions, curiosity, and even my doubt. Help me lean on you even when my heart is unsure and wants to keep away. You are bigger than my doubt. I believe, Lord; help my unbelief.

COMPELLED BY COMPASSION

"My heart goes out to this crowd, for they've already been here with me for three days with nothing to eat."
MARK 8:2 TPT

Before Jesus performed the miracle of feeding thousands, he felt compassion for them. This compassion compelled him to act. They had come to hear Jesus speak about the kingdom of heaven and their loving Father, and Jesus could demonstrate the love and care of the Father by feeding them.

How often do we act out of obligation rather than compassion? What if we left room in our hearts for love to move us? Jesus had spent three days teaching thousands of people, and they had nothing to eat. He showed both the power of God and the kindness of his mercy by blessing what food there was and having the disciples distribute it. After the people had been miraculously fed, he sent them on their way. Before you go on your way, let the compassion of Christ meet you to satisfy your hunger and ready you for what's ahead.

Jesus, just as you were moved by compassion to feed those who followed you, meet my needs with the love of your presence today. I rely on you, and I will follow in your footsteps.

WITH A LITTLE

He was asking them,
"How many loaves do you have?"
And they said, "Seven."
MARK 8:5 NASB

God takes what we have and multiplies it. Notice the partnership here. Jesus did not make bread appear from heaven (though God did this with the Israelites in the desert by providing manna). Instead, he took what was already available, blessed it, and it was multiplied.

Are you waiting for a miracle to appear out of thin air? Perhaps you have the beginnings of one already. Offer Jesus what you have, bless it, and follow his directions. Many times, we wait around for something to happen when Jesus asks us to play a part in its creation. Take stock, get up, and follow his directions.

Christ, you are the God who multiplies what little there is until there is more than enough. I don't want to wait around when you ask for my participation. Bless my little, Lord, and multiply it to meet the needs of others as well as my own.

IN OUR MIDST

Being asked by the Pharisees when the kingdom of God
would come, he answered them, "The kingdom of God
is not coming in ways that can be observed, nor will
they say, 'Look, here it is!' or 'There!' for behold,
the kingdom of God is in the midst of you."
LUKE 17:20-21 ESV

The people of Jesus' day were expecting the Messiah
to come and establish a governmental kingdom to rule
and reign as physical king over Israel. They thought Jesus
would overturn the Roman Empire, but Jesus turned their
expectations upside down. Instead of building a physical
kingdom, Jesus said it was already established. Not only
that, but he also said it was "in the midst" of the people.

His kingdom is here, now, in our midst. Yes, he will come
back and set every physical wrong right in his justice and
mercy. He will not delay returning forever. We will dwell
with him in his kingdom. Still, that kingdom is a spiritual
kingdom already established. It dwells in us through his
Spirit. What a marvelous mystery!

King Jesus, you are the ruler of my heart and life. I submit
to your ways and follow the law of love on which your
kingdom is built. Show me how to serve your kingdom.

ETERNAL HOPE

"Very truly I tell you, whoever hears my word and believes
him who sent me has eternal life and will not be judged
but has crossed over from death to life."
JOHN 5:24 NIV

Jesus makes it clear what is required of us if we want to
dwell in the realm of his eternal kingdom. If we listen to
Christ and believe the Father sent him, we enter into the
fullness of relationship with God through him. Then, we
can live out this eternal hope.

What we truly believe, we practice. Our lifestyles reveal
the deeper values that guide our decisions. With this in
mind, take stock of what principles your life reflects right
now. Reflect without shame but with curiosity. Only when
we are honest with ourselves can we be intentional about
the changes that need to be made. Today is a perfect
opportunity to align not only our minds and hearts with
Christ but also our habits.

Jesus, you are the way, the truth, and the life. Show me
where I am not living in your love and give me courage
to make changes that reflect the ways of your kingdom.

CONNECTION TO THE FATHER

"This is the way to have eternal life—to know you, the only true God, and Jesus Christ, the one you sent to earth."
JOHN 17:3 NLT

In prayer, Jesus took the time to mention the beauty and power of knowing and experiencing God. Not only is it a joy and a gift; it's the way to eternal life. Having a deep understanding, a true relationship with God the Father and Jesus Christ the Son, is the power of God's life within us.

How important is personal connection to God to your faith? How well do you know Jesus? There is always more to discover, greater revelation to reach, and deeper fellowship to cultivate. With the help of the Holy Spirit, you can prioritize your relationship with God and listen to him, learn from his Word, and offer him access to your heart. As we do, he will correct us with kindness, break through our limits with his love, and instruct us in his perfect wisdom.

Wise Jesus, thank you for revealing the purpose of your coming. You show us the way to eternal life. I want to know you more, experience the Father's love in greater measure, and grow with the transforming power of your Spirit.

SAY WHAT YOU MEAN

"Say only yes if you mean yes, and no if you mean no.
If you say more than yes or no, it is from the Evil One."
MATTHEW 5:37 NCV

There is power in honesty. When we say what we mean and follow through on what we say, nothing can trap us. We don't need to appease others with what we think they want to hear. It's more honorable to be true to our word.

Jesus knew the power of a promise, and he did not condone making a vow lightly. His kindness instructs us to be clear with our communication. It is a loving act, both for us and others, when we are clear about what we can and can't do. Embrace the beauty of clarity even if it means disappointing others. It would be greater trouble to say something we don't mean and not follow through on it later.

Jesus, all your teachings are based in kindness, goodness, and truth. Instead of writing off the wisdom of your Word, I want to live by it. Teach me to be clear and thoughtful in my communication and commitments.

PURSUIT OF PEACE

"You have heard that it was said, An eye for an eye and a tooth for a tooth. But I tell you, don't resist an evildoer. On the contrary, if anyone slaps you on your right cheek, turn the other to him also."

MATTHEW 5:38-39 CSB

God's ways are different from our human instincts. When someone strikes us, is it not our impulse to hit back? When we are under attack, don't we want to rally our defenses? Jesus gave a different directive. In John 15:13, Jesus summed up the power of humble love: "No one has greater love than this, to lay down one's life for his friends."

Today's verse goes a step further. We could probably imagine sacrificing our lives for those we love and who love us, but to not resist the attack of someone who doesn't like us is a level of love that Christ displayed first. He calls us to follow his example and trust the Father with the rest. We can promote peace in how we handle criticism and hate from others.

Jesus, your love is bigger, more patient, and more powerful than any I could muster on my own. I join with your purposes in pursuing peace, and I lay down my rights to get even. I trust you.

Among the Living

> "You are deluded because your hearts are not filled with the revelation of the Scriptures or the power of God… God is not the God of the dead, but of the living, and you are all badly mistaken!"
>
> Mark 12:24,27 tpt

What good is religion if it is for the dead but not the living? The hope of eternal life is wonderful, but what about the transformative power of God's life within us now? If all we have to look forward to is death, where is the joy of God's promises? Where is the peace of his presence? Where is the comfort of his love?

We need a God who is with us now, and he is. He promises to never leave or forsake those who look to him. He promises to strengthen, uphold, heal, and comfort the needy when they call on him. We need a faith rooted in our lived reality and not just the promise of a better reality to come. We need both. The revelation of the Scriptures and the power of God are for us to experience here and now, and they bring hope for what is to come.

Jesus, I want to know the power of your life in mine. I don't want to scrape by each day. My heart is yours; fill it with the revelation of your power.

ASTONISHING FAITH

When Jesus heard these things, He marveled at him, and
turned around and said to the crowd that followed Him,
"I say to you, I have not found such great faith,
not even in Israel!"

LUKE 7:9 NKJV

We do not need a legacy of Christianity or a lifetime of
understanding to believe in Jesus and take him at his
word. In fact, this interaction between Jesus and a Roman
captain is a wonderful illustration of remarkable faith.

The captain knew what the chain of command looked like,
and he also recognized the glory of Jesus and the lack of
his own goodness. Instead of asking Jesus to come to his
home, he asked that Jesus give the command from where
he currently stood. He knew his servant would be healed
instantly. That's what Jesus marveled at: this belief that
at Jesus' word, healing would be released. Compare this
to Thomas' doubt that required he stick his hand in the
wounds of Jesus to believe he was resurrected from the
dead. What kind of faith do we lean toward?

King Jesus, your word is filled with authority. May
my faith mirror captain who believed that what you
commanded would happen. Increase my confidence
as I walk in faith.

PROMOTED BY GOD

"Everyone who exalts himself will be humbled,
and the one who humbles himself will be exalted."
LUKE 14:11 NASB

When we remain humble before God and others, we
slow down when others may tend to overwork to draw
attention to themselves. God sees what we do both in
private and in public, and every bit of it counts. It is better
that God promote us instead of trying to prove ourselves
to others.

What is ours to focus on if not self-promotion or proving
ourselves? It is to do with integrity the work given to us.
Treat others the way you want to be treated. Be kind,
follow through on your word, and pursue peace. Let
your lifestyle be one no one can argue with, for you have
nothing to hide when you walk in the light of Christ's
kingdom. Let love lead and keep grace flowing. It is
human to err, but it is godly to extend mercy.

Jesus, keep me from striving for my place in this world
and fighting for the attention of others. I stand in the
confidence of who you say I am, and I will live humbly
before you and others.

PRESENCE OF PEACE

"It is I;
do not be afraid."
JOHN 6:20 ESV

The mere presence of Jesus is enough to bring peace. The disciples were in a boat in the middle of a large lake, and the wind and waves had picked up. Out of nowhere, they saw Jesus walking on the water toward them, but they didn't realize it was him. As soon as he told them who he was, they welcomed him into the boat, and they were transported to the other side of the lake.

Not only did the presence of Jesus bring peace and relief, but he also transported them at a pace they could not have accomplished on their own. When Jesus brings relief, he often takes the reins for a while. Do we trust that when we take Jesus in, he will bring us to where we need to be?

Lord, come to me in my time of need. I desperately need the peace of your presence. I open my heart and life to you, and I yield to your leadership. Do what only you can do, Lord.

JOYFUL JESUS

"The Son of Man came eating and drinking, and they say, 'Here is a glutton and a drunkard, a friend of tax collectors and sinners.' But wisdom is proved right by her deeds."

MATTHEW 11:19 NIV

"Wisdom is proved right by her deeds." In other words, those who walk in the wisdom of God's ways display it through their lives. How seriously do we embrace the wisdom of Christ? No matter what others say about us, the criticisms they throw, or the judgments they make, the fruit of our lives is evidence of what we value.

You might read this text and take it to mean we should appear perfect according to certain standards, so let's take a look at the context. Jesus was being criticized for celebrating feasts with friends and drinking wine. All the while, his criticizers were ignoring the miracles of love that Christ was doing and living. We can live in the freedom of the love of Christ and let his mercy guide us even when others complain or disagree.

Merciful Jesus, I love that you feasted and drank with friends. You celebrated with those who were rejoicing! May I not avoid times of celebration with those who rejoice. You are a joyful God.

DISTRACTING DETAILS

"Why all this fussing over forgetting to bring bread?
Do you still not see or understand what I say to you?
Are your hearts still hard?"
MARK 8:17 TPT

The disciples were confused by Jesus' warning in an earlier verse to be on their guard against the "yeast" of the Pharisees. They thought he was chastising them for not bringing bread. How often we misunderstand the words of Jesus! Still, he is kind and patient with us. He teaches us so we will grow in our understanding. Even as he corrects the disciples, he has the heart of a teacher.

Instead of jumping to conclusions in our confusion, we can ask the Lord for clarification. He brings perspective to our cloudy thoughts. We don't always read him right, and it's important to recognize this so we remain humble and teachable. Soften your heart to the Lord and his voice. Listen to understand and not just hear. His wisdom enlightens hearts, and his Spirit brings revelation to minds.

Wise Jesus, I don't want to get caught up on details you have already moved on from. Keep me from getting distracted by things that don't matter. Open the ears of my heart to know you more.

FREED FROM BONDAGE

When Jesus saw her, he called her over and said,
"Dear woman, you are healed of your sickness!"
LUKE 13:12 NLT

Jesus has compassion on us. He doesn't only deal with physical bonds or problems; he sees what keeps us stuck in bondage, and he calls us to himself. He frees us from our torment and delivers us from debilitating fear. In John 8:36, Jesus says, "So if the Son sets you free, you are truly free."

Jesus came to seek and save the lost. He came to set the captives free. He is the Redeemer and the one who came to set wrong things right. He was sent to release God's people from their spiritual prison. Whatever keeps us from the liberty of his love, he beckons us come and bring to him today. He is our liberator and our healer.

Mighty Healer, thank you for setting me free from sin, fear, torment, and oppression. You are better than any other. I run to you today. Wash over me with your kindness, Jesus, and free me from what keeps me stuck.

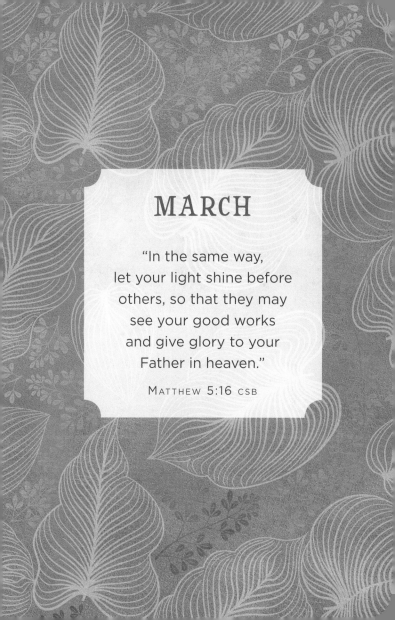

MARCH

"In the same way,
let your light shine before
others, so that they may
see your good works
and give glory to your
Father in heaven."

Matthew 5:16 CSB

PLENTY OF ROOM

"There are many rooms in my Father's house;
I would not tell you this if it were not true.
I am going there to prepare a place for you."
JOHN 14:2 NCV

God's kingdom is not small, and it is not only for an exclusive few. Jesus said he would go and prepare a place for us. He wasn't just speaking of his disciples; he includes all who would believe in him as the Son of God. This includes you! May we never tire of sharing God's love with others, for there is more room in his glorious kingdom than we can imagine.

God is bigger and better than we can imagine him to be. What a reason to let our hearts hope! What an encouragement to dream bigger, love more generously, and live with his joy and goodness on our lips and in our choices.

Son of God, you are preparing a place in your kingdom for me. May I never close my doors to those you welcome in with open arms. May I be hospitable, kind, and generous knowing that is what you would do.

GRACIOUS ASSURANCE

Jesus came up and touched them, and said,
"Get up; don't be afraid."
MATTHEW 17:7 CSB

One touch from the Lord is enough to give assurance
and fill us with courage. The disciples had just witnessed
a cloud of glory overshadow them, and they heard the
voice of the Father saying, "This is my Son, the Beloved;
with him I am well pleased; listen to him" (17:5). They were
understandably overwhelmed and afraid.

Was Jesus' response to let them shake under the fear?
No. He lifted them up, reassured them, and gave them
courage. When we are overcome, Jesus does the same for
us. He calls us to rise and not be afraid. May we walk in the
assurance of his presence and listen to him every step of
the way.

Son of God, your presence brings courage, comfort,
and peace. I will follow you. I will listen to all you have
already said and what you still speak today. You are my
God, my guide, and my teacher. I trust you.

COME AND REST

"Come aside by yourselves to a deserted place and rest a while." For there were many coming and going, and they did not even have time to eat.

MARK 6:31 NKJV

Has the pace of life drained you? There are always more tasks than there is time. Jesus doesn't expect you to burn out while serving others. He invites you to come to a place where there are no demands. He invites you to rest with him.

Do you resist taking time for yourself? Do you prioritize the needs of others so much that you neglect your own? You need nourishment, rest, and play as much as anyone else. You don't have to prove your love by neglecting yourself. That is a sure way to resentment and exhaustion. Take time to rest. Don't let the "shoulds" of life or the unending needs of others keep you from taking the time necessary to refresh and regroup. Take Jesus' offer and come aside by yourself to a deserted place and rest awhile.

Lord, thank you for loving me well. Thank you for reminding me that rest is not a luxury but a necessity. I will take the time to rest instead of overwork.

SPONTANEOUS PRAISE

He rejoiced greatly in the Holy Spirit, and said, "I praise
You, Father, Lord of heaven and earth, that You have
hidden these things from the wise and intelligent and
have revealed them to infants. Yes, Father, for doing so was
well pleasing in Your sight."

LUKE 10:21 NASB

Jesus rejoiced at the return of his disciples. They reported
their amazement over how they walked in the miracles
and power of Jesus even when they were out on their
own. Their awe and joy filled Jesus with joy too.

When was the last time someone's breakthrough filled you
with joy? It's important to remain connected to others in
love to rejoice when they rejoice and mourn when they
mourn. When you feel joy, lean into it. Jesus did. He gave
spontaneous praise to the Father from a heart overflowing
in gratitude. May you do the same and not rush to move
on from it.

Joyful Jesus, I give you praise for the way your merciful
miracles are still breaking through in people's lives. Give
me eyes to see, ears to hear, and a heart that perceives
your glorious power in the people around me. May their
joy be my own.

GOOD PORTION

The Lord answered her, "Martha, Martha, you are anxious
and troubled about many things, but one thing is
necessary. Mary has chosen the good portion, which will
not be taken away from her."
Luke 10:41-42 esv

While Martha worried about everything that needed to
be tended to in the household, Mary chose to sit at the
feet of Jesus and listen to him. She understood that the
work would always be there, but Jesus would not. When
we take the time to listen to Jesus as he speaks, we choose
the better portion.

Responsibility, hard work, and follow-through are all
good attributes. However, do they matter if our hearts
are not connected to the love of Christ? They have their
impact, but the reward soon passes. We must embrace
moments when the Spirit calls us to something that feels
unproductive and counterintuitive. The work will be there
when we return.

Jesus, I choose to follow your lead, listen to your
voice, and soak up the beauty of your presence today.
Household chores and to-do lists will still be here when I
get back. Help me prioritize your presence.

SOUL'S SATISFACTION

Jesus declared, "I am the bread of life.
Whoever comes to me will never go hungry,
and whoever believes in me will never be thirsty."
JOHN 6:35 NIV

Just as God the Father provided manna for Moses and the Israelites wandering in the desert, so he provided the satisfying bread of life in his Son, Jesus. When we come to him every day and consume the portion of his presence offered, we will not hunger. This is a divine satisfaction of the soul that fills our hearts, minds, and bodies. Jesus is also the thirst-quenching water for our souls, and our spiritual thirst is satisfied.

In him, all our needs are met, for he is the perfect portion. Don't neglect the power of his presence in your life; embrace the Son of God and his eternal bread and water. There is more than enough to satisfy.

Bread of Life, I come to you today with hunger in my heart and thirst in my soul. Satisfy me with the richness of your presence and bring nourishment, clarity, and peace to my inner being.

EMBRACED BY LOVE

"Those the Father has given me will come to me,
and I will never reject them."
JOHN 6:37 NLT

Jesus promises he will never turn away someone who comes to him. When we believe in Christ the Son and turn to him for wisdom, direction, and our identity as children of God, we are embraced by love. Does this mean we come to him perfectly? No. He perfects us by covering us in his gracious mercy. In him, we are made whole.

Have you been keeping your distance from Jesus? Do you hesitate to come to him? Do your questions, doubts, or longings make you feel as if you don't deserve his love? Nothing can separate you from his mercy, so don't let your excuses keep you away. He is standing with open arms ready to embrace you as you are.

Merciful One, thank you for not requiring perfection from me even when I am tempted to think you do. I will not stay away from you today; please wrap me up in your love.

BEYOND SACRIFICE

"If only you could learn the meaning of the words
'I want compassion more than a sacrifice,'
you wouldn't be condemning my innocent disciples."
MATTHEW 12:7 TPT

Compassion is greater than ceremony in the kingdom of Christ. Tradition is beneficial to a point, but it loses its meaning when it keeps us from expanding in love toward others. Christ was and is compelled by compassion. Are we? Or do we let the expectations of others keep us from following his example?

When faced with the opportunity, may we choose compassion over the religious expectations that confine us. Jesus broke barriers everywhere he went; why do we expect him to prefer those barriers today? Follow the leading of love even when it's uncomfortable. Prioritize compassion over rituals. The love of God is living and active just as his Word is.

Compassionate One, I have made many excuses to keep compassion from pulling me out of my comfort zone. Those excuses stop today. I choose to let your love lead instead of keeping myself behind barriers of religious rites.

UNITY OF LOVE

Jesus knew what the Pharisees were thinking,
so he said to them, "Every kingdom that is
divided against itself will be destroyed.
And any city or family that is
divided against itself will not continue."
MATTHEW 12:25 NCV

After reading the thoughts of the Pharisees who were convinced Jesus was driving out demons by the power of Satan, Jesus replied with today's verse. Setting people free from the bondage of fear, sickness, and torment can never be a work of the enemy. As Jesus said, a kingdom divided against itself will be destroyed.

This is applicable to the church of Christ too. If we are divided against each other in purpose, we will crumble under thrown accusations. Love unites where pride divides. May we remain humble in love and let it rule over every issue.

Jesus Christ, I am guilty of letting my opinions keep me from loving my brothers and sisters in your kingdom. A kingdom divided against itself cannot stand. Help me keep the banner of your love as my guidepost.

LAY IT DOWN

Calling the crowd along with his disciples, he said to them, "If anyone wants to follow after me, let him deny himself, take up his cross, and follow me."
MARK 8:34 CSB

Surrender is necessary to follow Christ. We must be willing to give up habits, preferences, and judgments. We need to let go of those chips on our shoulders to forgive and move toward mercy instead of away from it. This path of love that Christ calls us on isn't the easiest path to follow, but it's worth it.

Have we really laid down our rights to our comfort and getting even? Have we truly surrendered to Jesus' leadership? If we have, our hearts remain humble and open. We allow the teachings and example of Christ to transform us and challenge us. We can't stay the same when we follow him. Lay down your resistance, and let his love lead you. No matter how hard it gets, he will not leave you.

Loving Leader, I lay down my life and follow you. I surrender to your ways, and I give up my hold on my comfort. You know better than I do. I trust you.

CHECK YOUR HEART

"You are those who justify yourselves before men, but God knows your hearts. For what is highly esteemed among men is an abomination in the sight of God."

LUKE 16:15 NKJV

It does not matter how spiritual we appear to others if our hearts are not submitted to God. If we hurl judgments at others in the name of God, we may seem very religious, but we are missing the point altogether. God leads in mercy, and we follow his lead.

It's important to be aware of our hearts. When we check in with the motivations behind why we say, think, feel, and do certain things, we have the opportunity to change. If we assume our motivations are pure, we may be fooling ourselves. We unconsciously pick up and assign meaning and attributes to God that aren't based in his character or Word. May we remain humble and teachable: ready to change course, admit when we are wrong, and ask for forgiveness.

Jesus, your opinion of me matters more than others' opinions. It matters more than what I have been taught is right and wrong. You are the one who sees, knows, and judges rightly. I leave that to you. Transform me in the power of your mercy.

GRACE IN THE WORLD

*"I am not asking You to take them out of the world,
but to keep them away from the evil one."*
JOHN 17:15 NASB

We are not called to live secluded from the world. There is no reason to build communes or kingdoms of our own making. We are in the world to live, work, and relate to all types of people. Our hearts can stay pure in the love of Christ even while we interact with those who don't know him.

We can't be influential if we are removed from the world. We must take our places in the kingdom of God and in the spheres of influence we inhabit. We should not run from these things but embrace them. We do this by spending time with the Lord each day, inviting him to transform us, and allowing him to move through us as we live with integrity, purpose, and compassion.

Gracious Jesus, I join with your prayer to the Father and ask that you keep me from evil. Keep me from hatred, indifference, and judgment. May I be known for my love as it reflects your love in my life.

PERFECTLY ONE

"I in them and you in me, that they may become perfectly
one, so that the world may know that you sent me
and loved them even as you loved me."
JOHN 17:23 ESV

The Father lived fully in Jesus, and he lives fully in us
through the Spirit of God. This is what perfect unity looks
like: the love of the Triune God shining through us. May
we not hold so tightly to our preferences that we limit the
working wisdom of Christ in us. We must not tire of doing
good but instead do it all the more with purpose, grace,
and generosity.

How different would it be if God's character shined
through your choices? Perhaps the values of Christ's
kingdom are already your guiding values. Don't become
complacent; look for the binds that keep you from the
generosity of God's living mercy. May you find yourself
perfectly one with Father, Son, and Spirit. Submit to him,
and you will find the grace to choose his ways.

Jesus, thank you for the power of your love at work in
my heart, life, and relationships. I lay down my defenses.
Spirit, show me where I have yet to submit to you. I want
to reflect your generosity and compassion clearly.

SIGNIFICANT TO HIM

"Are not two sparrows sold for a penny? Yet not one of them will fall to the ground outside your Father's care."
MATTHEW 10:29 NIV

Nothing in this world escapes the notice of the Creator. Jesus said no sparrow falls to the ground without the Father's knowledge. If the Father cares for small birds that others don't pay attention to, how much more does he care for those he created in his image? We were made to reflect the nature of God.

Lay down your worries, big and small, about the details of your life. You don't have to ignore them; simply hand them over to Jesus. God knows what we need before we know to ask for it. We can trust his heart, power, and character to care for us when we are in need. Nothing is too insignificant for him.

Lord, I come with all my worries including the small, seemingly insignificant things. I want to trust you more than I worry about the details of my life. Take the weight of my worries and lead me into the fullness of your liberating love.

TRUTH OVER TRADITION

"You cancel the word of God in order to hand down your own tradition. And this is only one example among many others."
MARK 7:13 NLT

Jesus often reprimanded the Pharisees and religious scholars who defended manmade traditions over the law of God. Before we judge them too harshly, we should keep in mind the rules, traditions, and expectations we have of godly people. How much is rooted in the law of love Jesus preached? Whatever leads us away from compassion, denies responsibility for being kind and generous, causes division, or excuses our lack of love is most likely rooted in tradition rather than in the Word of God.

Before we rush to judge others, let's consider the words of Jesus when he said, "the standard you use in judging is the standard by which you will be judged" (Matthew 7:2). If we will be treated as we treat others, should we not be quick in mercy and slow in condemnation? Should we not be humble and understanding?

Jesus, I don't want to hold my understanding over your truth. I want to know the meaning of your truth and adjust my life accordingly instead of justifying my actions by manipulating your Word.

OUR CENTER

Jesus taught them this prayer: "Our heavenly Father, may the glory of your name be the center on which our life turns. May your Holy Spirit come upon us and cleanse us. Manifest your kingdom on earth."

LUKE 11:2 TPT

When we set the glory of God's name at our center, we make his opinion the sun around which we orbit. His truth becomes our anchor. We are grounded by his nature, Word, and power. This is the beginning of Jesus' teaching on prayer; we center our lives, hearts, and attention around the glory of the Father.

Before we move on with the day, let's focus our hearts on this basic truth. The Father is full of glory, love, and power. His ways are truer, wiser, and kinder than the world's. We look first to him and allow his perspective and holiness to wash over us. Then, we join with his heart and ask his Spirit to wash over us and bring the reality of his kingdom to earth.

Wise Teacher, thank you for taking the time to teach us how to pray. Heavenly Father, may the glory of your name be the center on which my life turns. I look to you.

SPIRIT AND TRUTH

"The time is coming when the true worshipers will worship the Father in spirit and truth, and that time is here already. You see, the Father too is actively seeking such people to worship him."

JOHN 4:23 NCV

Worship is not defined by where we are geographically. It is not something that must be done through rites in a church, temple, or other designated sacred space. To worship God in spirit and in truth is to worship him with our lives and obey his Word. No matter where we are, we offer God the worship of our surrendered hearts.

Have you ever considered that mundane tasks, when done with an attitude of submission and love, can be an expression of worship? That turns doing the dishes, buying groceries, cooking meals, switching out the laundry, going on walks, and more into opportunities to worship the Lord in spirit and truth. We can intentionally turn our attention to the Lord throughout the day and offer him the surrender of our love.

Jesus, I want to worship you in spirit and in truth. Fill me with the power of your Spirit as I turn my heart to your presence in humble awe. Meet me in the mundane today.

SHARE

"They don't need to go away," Jesus told them.
"You give them something to eat."
MATTHEW 14:16 CSB

Jesus taught that true leadership and care is not only about feeding the soul but also feeding the person. It is not enough to offer words of encouragement. If people are hungry, we share what we have and feed them. To be generous with what we have is a major part of the kingdom of Christ.

The disciples did not have vast resources of food when Jesus gave this instruction, but by giving thanks and blessing the loaves and fish, a miracle was born. The food did not run out as they distributed it to the crowd of thousands. When others are hungry and we have something to share, instead of looking at the scarcity of our resources, we can bless it and rely on the Lord's goodness to multiply our offering.

Generous Jesus, I don't want to overlook the power of sharing my resources with others. You told your disciples to feed the hungry among them. Help me do the same.

EVERY CREATURE

"Go into all the world
and preach the gospel to every creature."
MARK 16:15 NKJV

When Jesus appeared to his disciples after his resurrection, he first corrected them for not believing the testimony of others who had seen him already. Instead of embracing the good news, they resisted it. Still, after correcting them, he directed them to spread the news of the gospel to everyone.

Every person, no matter who they are, where they come from, or what life they lead, is meant to hear the wonderful news of Christ's ministry, death, and resurrection. The power of his life is for all who believe and not only those we think are worthy. Every person is a unique reflection of God. God's desire is for all to hear and respond to his invitation, so don't resist sharing the good news of Christ with anyone.

Jesus, if others don't hear your invitation, how will they know to come? I want to share your love freely and openly. Make me brave enough to do it.

WHAT FAITH IS ABOUT

"Truly I say to you, whoever does not receive the kingdom
of God like a child will not enter it at all."
LUKE 18:17 NASB

Why does Jesus say we must receive the kingdom of God
like a child to enter it? What traits do children possess that
we lose as adults? The faith of a child is simple and not
easily broken. They take people at their word and don't
doubt that those who instruct them know what they are
talking about. They only learn to be skeptical after being
tricked many times.

Faith is built on loving trust. We rely on the unwavering
nature of the Father, take him at his Word, and build our
lives on him. Jesus does not manipulate, control, or fool us.
He doesn't play games with our trust. He is worthy of our
faith because he is the way, the truth, and the life. May our
childlike innocence bloom in the light of his steadfast love.

Lord, I trust you because you are trustworthy. You are
who you say you are. Thank you for not holding my
doubts against me; you are so patient. Increase my faith
as you follow through on your Word.

LOVING OBEDIENCE

"You are my friends
if you do what I command you."
JOHN 15:14 ESV

Obedience to Jesus' words and teachings reflects our relationship to him. If we trust Jesus is the Son of God, revealing the heart of the Father, why would we ignore his directions? He is the wisdom of God in human form; he experienced everything we go through. If he isn't trustworthy, who is?

Jesus called his disciples friends and not servants. He gave them direction, but he also taught them what the Father had revealed. Servants don't always understand their employer, but Jesus shared with his friends what the Father was doing. He still calls us friends, and he gives his Spirit to bring power and perspective to our lives. We offer him our obedience in return.

Wise Jesus, thank you for sharing the heart of the Father and not just giving rules and regulations without explanation. Everything you shared was rooted in the nature of God, and it is my honor and delight to be your friend and live by your example.

COURAGE TO SPEAK

One night, the Lord spoke to Paul in a supernatural vision and said, "Don't ever be afraid. Speak the words that I give you and don't be intimidated, because I am with you. No one will be able to hurt you, for there are many in this city whom I call my own."

ACTS 18:9-10 TPT

Sometimes, direct encouragement from the Lord is exactly what we need. The reassurance that God's presence will never leave us, and he will give us right words to say, is a relief. When God calls us to something, he equips us, and he promises to be with us through it all.

Receive the words of Christ in your present season. Reread the verse for today through the lens of Jesus speaking directly to you. He is with you; have no fear. He will give you the words you need at the right moment. Don't be intimidated by others, for the powerful presence of God is at work within and through you. Invite the Spirit to minister directly to your heart as you receive the kindness of Jesus through his Word.

Jesus, thank you for your promise to never leave us. Refresh me in your presence so I may have courage to continue in the way that you have called me.

POWERFUL GRACE

"My grace is sufficient for you,
for my power is made perfect in weakness."
2 Corinthians 12:9 NIV

When Paul speaks of his prayer life, it gives us a glimpse into the conversations he has with the Lord. When we follow the Lord and submit to him, we also can have this open fellowship with the Spirit.

Paul pleaded with the Lord to remove a thorn from him. While we don't know what that thorn was, instead of relieving him, God said, "My grace is sufficient for you." It's difficult when God says we must persevere when we want relief, but God's power is made perfect in our weakness. When we have nothing left to offer, there is more room for his power to move in and through us. We can embrace God's answer even when it's not the answer we were looking for. Trust his character and receive the strength of his grace.

Gracious Jesus, even when you don't answer my prayers the way I want, your power can shine through my weakness. Your will be done, Lord; I am yours.

BEGINNING AND END

When I saw him, I fell at his feet as if I were dead.
But he laid his right hand on me and said,
"Don't be afraid! I am the First and the Last."
REVELATION 1:17 NLT

Jesus is the first and last, the beginning and the end. He was there in the beginning, and he will be through every generation. There is no time and space where he is not. It's hard to wrap our heads around, but it's true. With this reality in mind, let's meditate on his relentless presence that does not leave or waver.

The love of God is his very nature. Where the Lord is, there is overflowing mercy. Instead of letting fear push us to self-protect or lash out, we can grab hold of the peace of Christ that settles our fears and gives us courage to walk with him. He never changes, and he never will. He is the same from age to age. He can't be contained by people's misgivings or misunderstandings of his character. He is powerfully persistent in merciful kindness, and his throne is built on righteous truth.

Alpha and Omega, instead of judging you by the changing opinions in this world, I look to you as the foundation, standard, and goal. Thank you for relieving my fear and calling me your own.

HE IS ALIVE

"I am the One who lives;
I was dead, but look, I am alive forever and ever!
And I hold the keys to death and to the place of the dead."
REVELATION 1:18 NCV

Jesus, in describing who he is to John in this vision, includes the fact that he was once dead. Though he was crucified, dead, and buried, he was resurrected to life and now lives forever. He will never sleep or fall silent. He has victory over death and the grave, and he holds the keys to unlock the unseen world.

In short, all authority over death belongs to Jesus Christ. We have no reason to fear because his resurrection is our triumph too. We come alive in his life-giving light. In these mortal bodies, we experience the renewal of our souls in his Spirit, but when he comes again, we will receive our forever bodies that will never decay or fall ill. A glorious reality lies ahead.

King Jesus, you are alive! In your eternal kingdom, I will experience the beauty of your glorious life forever. Thank you for this wonderful promise.

TIGHT GRIP

"Whoever wants to save his life will lose it, but whoever loses his life for My sake and the gospel's will save it."
MARK 8:35 NASB

To fully follow Jesus, we can't hold too tightly to our lives. Our resources are only ours for a short time. When we live in a mindset of generosity rather than scarcity, there is no reason to hold tightly. God has given us gifts; we can be generous with what we have been given.

What does it mean to choose to keep our lives for ourselves? Jesus answers this in the following verse (8:36): "For what does it benefit a person to gain the whole world, and forfeit his soul?" In other words, wealth and power mean nothing in the kingdom of God. While those with wealth and power can influence governments, economies, and cultures, they can't bribe the heart of God. The most important thing we can guard is our souls. How do we do this? By surrendering to the leadership of Christ no matter how much pride or position we need to sacrifice.

Jesus, your wisdom is better than the world's. You are not impressed by prestige, power, or wealth. You look at our hearts. My heart is yours, Lord. I offer you all I have because you are worth it.

RIGHT FOCUS

"When the Son of Man comes in his glory, and all the
angels with him, then he will sit on his glorious throne."
MATTHEW 25:31 CSB

Jesus is coming again. He will come in all his glory with
the angels. He will sit on his glorious throne with all the
nations gathered before him. From that place, he will
judge every person based on their lives and hearts.

It is not our place to judge one another. It is Christ's, and
he will do it rightly. He alone knows the heart of every
person. He sees what others don't bother to notice.
He sees the sacrifices of love hidden from our eyes. He
recognizes the pride of a person's cold-heartedness even
when everyone around them raves about how charming
they are. It's not our place to judge. It's our duty to tend to
our gardens by planting seeds of love, joy, peace, patience,
and kindness, which will bear fruit in our actions.

Jesus, I want to keep first things first. I don't want to be
distracted by offense or criticism that leads me away
from my responsibilities. Keep my heart centered on
what is mine to do and mine to offer.

Accessible Revelations

"I praise you, Father, Lord of heaven and earth, because you have hidden these things from the wise and learned, and revealed them to little children."
MATTHEW 11:25 NIV

God delights in revealing himself to those who seek him. His wisdom is not reserved for the educated; it is readily accessible to all who trust him and follow his instructions. He uses what seems to be weak by world standards to shame the wise (1 Corinthians 1:27). He gladly meets the willing hearts.

Is pride keeping us from fully grasping the wisdom of Christ? Do we think we know better than God? We must refresh our childlike faith. Then, we can chase after the Lord with all our hearts, souls, and minds and love him with our whole lives. He is worthy of our trust, surrender, and worship.

Wise One, I don't have to be dressed up, in a good mental space, or free from all distraction to find you. I come to you as I am with an open and humble heart. Thank you for coming to me as I am.

NO MATTER WHAT

"Abba, Father, all things are possible for You.
Take this cup away from Me;
nevertheless, not what I will, but what You will."
MARK 14:36 NKJV

Jesus did not want to suffer. This is important for us to recognize. He was willing, yes, but he did not prefer it. Nobody wants to be in pain, and Jesus, in his frail human body, was no different. However, we can learn from his process and response.

Jesus saw what was ahead of him, and as the time of suffering drew near, he resisted it. He prayed that God would deliver him from it. He was honest. We don't have to pretend to be braver than we are. This is not where Jesus' prayer ended. In its beautiful conclusion, Jesus said, "nevertheless, not what I will, but what you will." When we lay out what we want from God, may we take the lead of Jesus and end it with surrender.

Abba, Father, all things are possible for you. You see my suffering. I don't want to go through any more pain. If you will, take it away from me. Nevertheless, not what I will, but what you will. Not what I want, but what you want. I trust you.

LASTING LIFE

"What does it benefit a person to gain the whole world, and forfeit his soul?"
MARK 8:36 NASB

There is abundance in the kingdom of heaven, and it is no consolation prize. When we choose to surrender to the leadership of Christ and follow his path of laid-down love, we choose the better way not only for this life but also for the kingdom to come.

When we surrender to Jesus, our souls are found in him. He brings us life everlasting and infuses our hearts with his peace, joy, love, and hope. There is more than enough grace to empower us to choose his ways over our own. We stay submitted; he leads us in the ways of his kingdom and offers us resources from the generosity of the Father. There is always more than enough in him even when others think we only have a little. Our souls thrive in the love of Christ, so let's seek him more than any earthly power or influence.

Worthy One, I don't want to lose myself by becoming consumed by my place in this world. I am found alive in your love. I want you more than I want a name for myself.

NO EXCUSES

"Love your enemies, and do good, and lend, expecting
nothing in return, and your reward will be great,
and you will be sons of the Most High, for he is
kind to the ungrateful and the evil."

LUKE 6:35 ESV

Where others put limits on their acts of generosity and
love, Christ removed them all. Though a good person will
give to a friend in need, who in their right mind would
offer anything to an enemy? According to Christ, an
enemy is as good as a friend when it comes to his love.
There are no barriers to his merciful kindness.

We should pay attention to where we, or others, draw
lines of distinction between who is worthy of our love
and generosity and who is not. In the kingdom of Christ, every
person receives the same measure. We are not exempt
from showing love to those who offend, hate, or ridicule
us; we are called to love them in the same way we love
those closest to us. When we dare to be generous with
compassion, we reflect the mercy of Christ.

Glorious Jesus, your ways are so different from those
who draw lines between themselves and others. You
broke down every barrier. Help me break my barriers too.

April

"Ask and it will be given to you.
Seek and you will find.
Knock, and the door
will be opened to you."

Matthew 7:7 csb

WHAT MATTERS MOST

"Why would you strive for food that is perishable and not be passionate to seek the food of eternal life, which never spoils? I, the Son of Man, am ready to give you what matters most, for God the Father has destined me for this purpose."

JOHN 6:27 TPT

We can't live without food. In the same way, our souls need the nourishment of God's presence to flourish and grow. In today's verse, Jesus isn't saying we should give up working to meet our physical needs. He is saying that since we do work, how much more should we diligently seek the nourishment of God's kingdom that never spoils?

Jesus readily offers what matters most. He does this for each of us as we come to him. Do we take our spiritual hunger as seriously as our physical hunger? If we do, we will pursue the presence of Christ, obey his Word, and live in his law of love. As we do, we are fed and sustained by the life of God within us. There is more than enough to satisfy; keep feeding on his goodness.

Bread of Life, thank you for your wonderful provision. I am nourished by your Word, refreshed by your presence, and satisfied by your love. Fill me up even more, Lord, so I may have more to offer to others.

LIGHT OF THE WORLD

"I am the light of the world. If you follow me,
you won't have to walk in darkness,
because you will have the light that leads to life."
JOHN 8:12 NLT

Jesus' invitation to walk in the light of his life, wisdom, and love is as much for us as it was for the people he originally spoke to. His invitation is for all who come to him. We don't have to walk in darkness; Christ is the light that leads to life.

Whatever area of your life feels cloudy or confusing, bring it to Jesus and watch him light it up with his perfect presence. He gives peace that passes understanding, and even when our minds can't comprehend what he is doing, we can still experience the power of his love lighting up our hearts like a fire. Why hesitate to follow him?

Liberating Light, thank you for meeting me with your powerful presence no matter where I am. I trust you to guide me step by step. Help me follow you.

A LITTLE GOES FAR

"The kingdom of heaven is like yeast that a woman took and
hid in a large tub of flour until it made all the dough rise."
MATTHEW 13:33 NCV

A little yeast is enough to affect a large amount of flour.
A tiny light can infiltrate the darkness. A seed of faith can
permeate a whole atmosphere. This is what Jesus says the
kingdom of heaven is like; a little goes a long way.

We don't need perfect faith. We don't have to have it
all figured out to follow the Lord. In fact, we can get
overwhelmed by the big picture and lose sight of the
practical steps needed to take to get there, if we are not
careful. Instead of waiting until we have all the steps
lined up, let's just take the steps we know to take today.
Little things done with consistency and love will lead to
big rewards.

Jesus, I don't have to have everything figured out to be
obedient. Clarify my next step, and I will take it. Thank
you for showing me the power in the little things.

EVEN MORE

"Whoever has, more will be given to him,
and whoever does not have,
even what he has will be taken away from him."
MARK 4:25 CSB

When we listen with open hearts to understand, we receive more revelation. If we remain closed off, however, what little we think we have will be lost. The truth of God is given to those who willingly receive it. Do we think we know all there is to know about God?

We need humility and curiosity to be open to teaching. Let us be like children who find joy in learning and growing. As we do, we will be given more, just as children are given more capacity to grow in their understanding as they delight in each new discovery and mastery of things once unattainable to them.

Teacher, I don't claim to know it all. In fact, the longer I live, I realize how little I actually know and how much more there is to discover. Increase my understanding as I delight in discovering more of your kingdom and your heart.

PREPARING WORDS

"Listen carefully to what I am about to tell you: The Son of
Man is going to be delivered into the hands of men."
LUKE 9:44 NIV

Jesus purposefully prepared his disciples for the day
he would be taken from them. Even though they could
not quite grasp what he was saying, he warned them. In
hindsight, they saw clearly what they could not comprehend
at the time. How often is that true of us as well?

When was the last time you looked through the lens
of hindsight and saw more clearly than you did in
the muddle of the moment? Emotions can cloud our
understanding, and our bias wills us to see what we want
to be true. We are not wrong to react this way; it's natural.
However, God gives us the grace to reflect on words that
prepare our hearts for the future.

Son of Man, thank you for speaking your words of
preparation even when I can't fully understand them
in the moment. Thank you for readying my heart.

RESURRECTION LIFE

"I am the resurrection and the life.
He who believes in Me, though he may die, he shall live."
JOHN 11:25 NKJV

Even when Jesus doesn't resurrect the bodies of those we love so we can have more time with them on earth, he promises we will live again with him if we believe he is the Son of God. He is the resurrection and the life; whoever believes in him will not cease to exist but will live forever in his kingdom.

What happens when we put our hope in this? When we realize the end of this small, short existence is not actually our end, we are free to live for what truly matters instead of trying to satisfy desires that may or may not be filled. We don't know how much time we have, but we can make the most of it by living for the kingdom of Christ while loving and caring for those we have the privilege of knowing.

Eternal One, you are the resurrection and the life, and I look to you for all I need and long for. Thank you for the eternal hope I have in you. This short life is not the end.

GLORY REVEALED

"Did I not say to you that if you believe,
you will see the glory of God?"
JOHN 11:40 NASB

When we believe in Jesus as the Son of God, it is inevitable we will see the glory of God in our midst. Just as Jesus told Martha she would see the glory of God and she watched her brother come back to life, so we will experience mighty miracles of God's mercy.

What has God spoken to you? Do you believe he will follow through? May expectation strengthen your heart with hope, and may you not grow tired of waiting for his power to show up. He is better than you can imagine, and he will not let even one of his promises be forgotten. He is always faithful to his word.

Lord Jesus, I long to see your glory, and I know it will probably require a test of my faith. Keep my heart open as I trust in you and pursue me with your passion when I begin to doubt. I love you, and I rely on you.

EVEN THE DEAD RESPOND

When he had said these things,
he cried out with a loud voice,
"Lazarus, come out."
JOHN 11:43 ESV

Before he called the lifeless body of Lazarus out of the tomb, Jesus prayed. He thanked the Father for hearing his prayer. He prayed for the benefit of those around him and said he would use the power the Father had given him. Jesus did this so there would be no mistake about where his power came from or whom Jesus had come from.

What happened? Lazarus stumbled out of his tomb with his grave clothes still wrapped around him. Can you imagine the faith, joy, astonishment, and awe that those with Jesus must have felt at witnessing this? Even the dead respond to Jesus' voice. May we offer him all we are, for he is worthy.

Messiah, there is no mistaking that you moved in spectacular power through your ministry. You even raised the dead! I want to know you more, marvelous Jesus. Fill my heart with faith.

PASSIONATE PURSUIT

"If you want to test my teachings and discover where I received them, first be passionate to do God's will, and then you will be able to discern if my teachings are from the heart of God or from my own opinions."
JOHN 7:17 TPT

Jesus was strategic when he told those who wanted to test his teachings that they must first be passionate to do God's will. Anyone can critique or criticize without surrendering to God or serving him. If we are not invested in finding solutions, our judgments are biased, and our hearts may remain closed off to understanding.

Passionate pursuit of God and his ways is the first step to truly knowing him. If we stay at a distance and only go to him when it's convenient, we miss out on much of what God has to offer. If we truly know the Lord, we understand his character and learn what his voice sounds like and what his presence feels like. Before we claim to know better, we must know the one who holds all wisdom.

Jesus, thank you for sharing your wisdom with us. I humble my heart, laying down my preconceived notions, and I pursue you and align my life with your ways.

ABUNDANT GROWTH

"The Kingdom of Heaven is like a mustard seed planted in a field. It is the smallest of all seeds, but it becomes the largest of garden plants; it grows into a tree, and birds come and make nests in its branches."

MATTHEW 13:31-32 NLT

The kingdom of heaven is planted like a small seed in our hearts, and when we allow it to take root within us, it grows exponentially. When we nurture the word of Christ, submitting to his leadership and following his ways, the kingdom expands in us.

The kingdom of Christ is more than what can be held, known, or experienced in any individual life. It is larger than the known world, and it is more powerful than any force used against humanity. The kingdom is a shelter for all who come to build their nests in it. It is a place of refuge and respite. As citizens of God's kingdom, may we be safe places for others to rest.

Lord Jesus, may your kingdom come and your will be done in my life on this earth. Increase the influence of your kingdom ways as I submit to you and grow abundantly.

OLD AND NEW TOGETHER

"Every teacher of the law who has been taught about the kingdom of heaven is like the owner of a house. He brings out both new things and old things he has saved."
MATTHEW 13:52 NCV

God is ancient. From the beginning, he was. He is present here and now. God will outlast every other being or power; he will be for all eternity. In him, the old and new belong together, so the instructions he gave to our ancestors are meant to instruct us now too.

God is still working and doing new things. There is room for both the old and the new to dwell together. We see this in how generations can work together. In the kingdom of heaven, everyone's place is important. Let's not throw away the wisdom our faith is built upon; it's our launching pad. They are meant to work together.

Timeless One, I don't want to neglect the wisdom already at work within my life and in your kingdom. Help me to appreciate the old and embrace the new as well.

LISTEN FIRST

"What are you arguing with them about?"
MARK 9:16 CSB

Instead of jumping into the middle of an argument with a lecture, Jesus asked, "What are you arguing about?" He first listened and gave them a chance to explain themselves. How often do we jump to conclusions instead of asking questions to understand before we offer perspective or advice? Jesus didn't storm in to put people in their place. Why would we?

It is worth our time, energy, and humility to carefully gauge a situation by checking in with those involved rather than making assumptions. We can follow the lead of Jesus and enter into spaces, especially ones with tensions running high, with open hearts to first listen and assess. Only then should we venture to respond.

Lord, thank you for your wise example. Help me refrain from jumping to conclusions without first listening to others. I want to be discerning and wise by taking time to understand others' viewpoints as best I can.

IMPORTANCE OF SERVICE

"Anyone who wants to be first must be the very last,
and the servant of all."

MARK 9:35 NIV

This directive was in response to the disciples arguing about which of them was the greatest. We all want favored places in the sight of others, don't we? It was no different for the disciples; they each wanted to be the best. However, Jesus said anyone who wants to be first must be willing to be the very last. He prescribed a humble, pliant attitude instead of a proud, pushy one.

How many of us take this truth to heart? If we want to be known as great, we must be willing to humble ourselves and let others go ahead of us. If we want to honor God with our lives, we must seek to serve all people. We can't pick and choose who is worthy of our generosity.

Jesus, your kingdom does not work the way this world does. I don't want to spend my time promoting myself when you are calling me to serve. Humble my spirit to be servant of all.

LOST AND FOUND

"What man of you, having a hundred sheep, if he loses one
of them, does not leave the ninety-nine in the wilderness,
and go after the one which is lost until he finds it?"
LUKE 15:4 NKJV

When we are responsible for living things, it is no small
problem when one of them goes missing. Who would not
go off to look for the lost one? In God's kingdom, those
who are lost are sought out. Jesus goes to find the ones in
the fringes and brambles. He does not let us wander so far
away that he can't find us.

No matter how lost you feel today, know that the Good
Shepherd comes after you. He has his eye on you. He
will gather you up, carry you back to the flock, and heal
your wounds. There is nowhere you can go that is away
from his presence. You can't wander your way outside of
his knowledge. Wherever you go, he finds you. You can't
outrun his love. Yield to his kindness today, for he tenderly
cares for you.

Good Shepherd, no one is outside the bounds of your
love. There is nowhere I can go to escape your presence.
What a wonderful relief that is. Wrap me up in your
compassion and refresh my heart in your living waters
of truth.

EMBRACED BY LOVE

"The young son set off for home. From a long distance away, his father saw him coming, dressed as a beggar, and great compassion swelled up in his heart for his son who was returning home. So the father raced out to meet him. He swept him up in his arms, hugged him dearly, and kissed him over and over with tender love."

LUKE 15:20 TPT

When the young son decided to return home, disgraced and ashamed, he didn't know how his father would receive him. He was ready to beg to be a servant. He didn't expect to be treated as a son because he had squandered away everything his father had given him. He was prepared to work alongside the employees.

The father's reaction to his son's return must have overwhelmed the young man. While the son was away from his father, shame told him he wasn't worthy of his father's compassion, but who could stop the father's love? This is how our heavenly Father receives us when we turn to him. He is full of affection and delight over our return.

Jesus, I can't begin to describe how needy I am. I come to you ready for anything today. Wash over me with your perfect love.

HOMECOMING

"The son said to him, 'Father, I have sinned against heaven and before you. I am no longer worthy to be called your son.' But the father said to his servants, 'Bring quickly the best robe, and put it on him, and put a ring on his hand, and shoes on his feet.'"

LUKE 15:21-22 ESV

Repentance is a beautiful act of surrender to the love of the Father. It admits we have done wrong and chooses to submit to whatever the Father has for us. We yield to his correction. We humble ourselves before him and allow him to do what he will.

Does the Father shame us when we come to our senses? Not at all. He clothes us with his own royal robes. Jesus has already offered all we need to be fully purified and made right in God's presence. We are covered in the garments of Christ, and he calls us his own. Who God says we are is more important than how we feel about ourselves, and he does not manipulate, humiliate, or destroy our hearts when we yield them to him.

Christ, I am most at home in your presence. You usher me into the Father's pure affection, and I am loved to life. Thank you for your indescribable kindness to me.

REASON TO REJOICE

"Son, you have always been with me, and all that is mine is yours. But we had to celebrate and rejoice, because this brother of yours was dead and has begun to live, and was lost and has been found."

LUKE 15:31-32 NASB

How do those of us who have faithfully served God react to the outpouring of love God has on those who were lost and are now found? How do we feel when people who were stuck in cycles of sin and destruction are liberated in his mercy? Perhaps we feel the way the older brother did: indignant and offended.

May we hear what the Father is saying in this verse. When we are in the kingdom of Christ, partnering with his purposes, all he has is also ours. We share in his abundance. Let's celebrate with the Father's heart by rejoicing with those who have returned home. Let's allow the love of our faithful Father increase our own. He is perfectly good, and there is reason to rejoice when he rejoices.

Jesus, keep my heart from bitterness and speak your words of life to redirect my perspective with your incomparable wisdom. I want to rejoice when you rejoice.

UNIMPRESSED

"I tell you the truth, it is very hard for a rich person to enter the Kingdom of Heaven. I'll say it again—it is easier for a camel to go through the eye of a needle than for a rich person to enter the Kingdom of God!"
MATTHEW 19:23-24 NLT

God is not influenced by people with power and prestige. A wealthy person can't buy their way into the kingdom of Christ. We enter into the kingdom of God with submission, humility, and faith. Before we are impressed with a person's status or lifestyle, consider what matters to God.

If we trust our resources or riches more than God, we will have a hard time sacrificing what we deem our safety net. What keeps us comfortable may serve us in this life, but it will not do anything to enrich our souls. May we be generous, kind, and gracious as we live for the age to come.

Jesus, help me choose you over my own comfort and preferences. I want to live for what truly matters and not hoard my wealth but generously love with my words and actions.

ONE AND THE SAME

"I have been with you a long time now. Do you still not know me, Philip? Whoever has seen me has seen the Father. So why do you say, 'Show us the Father'?"
JOHN 14:9 NCV

Jesus was a clear reflection of the Father; he still is today. Though he was a man experiencing the limits of humanity, he was also God and full of divine nature. Jesus said he only did what he saw the Father doing (John 5:19). The glory of God was all over Jesus, yet he was cloaked with humanity. Was this human form why Philip needed more proof?

Jesus was patient with Philip. He continues, "I tell you the truth, whoever believes in me will do the same things that I do. Those who believe will do even greater things than these, because I am going to the Father" (vs. 12). Instead of kicking Philip out of his trusted group of disciples, Jesus used it as a teaching opportunity. May we be unafraid to say what is on our hearts, and may we receive the truth of Christ as he corrects and encourages us.

Lord Jesus, I look to you, and as I do, I see the nature of the Father. Empower me in your Spirit and build my faith as I continually come to you.

ACTS OF COMPASSION

"I was hungry and you gave me something to eat; I was thirsty and you gave me something to drink; I was a stranger and you took me in; I was naked and you clothed me; I was sick and you took care of me; I was in prison and you visited me."

MATTHEW 25:35-36 CSB

Jesus says that when we act with practical compassion to meet others' needs, we are serving Jesus himself. Take some time to meditate on this wonderful truth. When we offer food to someone who is hungry, we can do it as if we are feeding Jesus. When we take care of the sick, welcome the stranger, and visit the lonely, each is an act of worship.

Does this change the way you look at such acts? Would it change how often you acted with practical kindness if you knew Jesus saw and received each one as if it were being done to him? Acts of compassion are not just good things to do; practices of kindness are our offering of worship to the Creator of all things.

Compassionate One, I am changed by your kindness in my life. I offer you not only words of worship but my lifestyle and choices as well. I will do good, act justly, and love mercy with my life.

OBEDIENT LOVE

"Anyone who loves me will obey my teaching.
My Father will love them, and we will come to them
and make our home with them."
JOHN 14:23 NIV

In our earthly relationships, compromise is an act of love. Jesus, who is perfect, asks us to submit to his ways. We can do this with confidence because he always has our best at heart, and he knows what he is doing. How do we show him love?

God makes his home in us when we lovingly make room for him. We can also show our love through our submission to Christ and his ways. This means laying down our rights to personal positions and preferences. True love is found in how we respond to the object of our affection. A love that is not responsive is not a true expression of God's love.

Lord Jesus, I love you more than words can say. My life reflects the depth of my love for you. I choose to trust you, follow you, and correct my feet when I veer off the path of your love. Make your home in me.

IN OUR STUBBORNNESS

"What did Moses command you?" They said, "Moses permitted a man to write a certificate of divorce, and to dismiss her." And Jesus answered and said to them, "Because of the hardness of your heart he wrote you this precept."
MARK 10:3-5 NKJV

This interaction between Jesus and the Pharisees illustrates how God meets us where we are. Jesus did not say that Moses went against God in allowing divorce, yet he makes it clear that divorce was never the intention of God. That hasn't changed; marriage is meant to be one-time only. Instead of building our arguments and lives on the exceptions, let's go back to the beginning: the foundation of our faith.

Are we stubbornly holding on to our beliefs about right and wrong? Are we immovable in our understanding, or is there enough of a teachable heart for God's truth to break through? He will meet us in any case, but we want to be transformed by his heart and trust his ways over our tendency to bend the rules.

God of Truth, it's a relief that you see my heart as it is. Teach me, mold me, and transform me in your wisdom.

WHAT ABOUT YOU

"Who do you say that I am?"
LUKE 9:20 NASB

Regardless of who others think Jesus is, who do you say he is? It's a question each of us must answer. Our parents can't do it for us; neither can our partners. Our friends can't carry our faith. We are seen and known for who we are and what we believe. Jesus will not overlook even one of us.

What you believe matters. It affects every area of your life. Your thoughts, actions, and intentions work together to produce a life built on your values. Take this opportunity to evaluate and choose how you want to live. The present moment is when the power of your choices matters. Don't put off for tomorrow what can be done today.

Jesus Christ, you are my Redeemer, my hope, and my closest friend. With you, much more is possible than I could achieve on my own. I want to know you more, reflect your love in my life, and live to honor your name.

BELOW THE SURFACE

A woman from Samaria came to draw water.
Jesus said to her, "Give me a drink."
JOHN 4:7 ESV

Jesus interacting with a woman from Samaria at the well may not seem like a big deal. During Jesus' time, however, addressing a Samaritan was a counter-cultural act. Jews and Samaritans had a long history of disagreements and dislike. Instead of sticking to rules and expectations, however, Jesus initiated a conversation with the woman. In the end, we know what happened. Jesus knew her heart. She was astonished to hear him speak confidently about her life, and he was right about all of it.

How often do we keep ourselves from reaching out to others because of expectations and societal norms? Let's follow Jesus' example and break down walls of class, gender, culture, and race. Jesus avoided no one, so we won't avoid interacting with others either.

Jesus, thank you for speaking with women, Samaritans, and Gentiles and ministering to them. You care about all people, and I want to be like you.

OASIS OF PEACE

"Are you weary, carrying a heavy burden?
Then come to me. I will refresh your life,
for I am your oasis."
MATTHEW 11:28 TPT

Every day has the possibility of taking on new, heavy burdens. There are diseases spreading, mental health crises happening, wars, rumors of wars, and the struggle to live in a world where prices and economic strain make it harder to get by. There are so many reasons to worry! And yet, Jesus says we can take our burdens to him. He promises to refresh us in the living waters of his presence.

Every time a burden weighs you down, come to Jesus. Give him the heavy load no matter how little or how long you have been carrying it. He will do the heavy lifting for you. He is a good God, a gracious friend, and a faithful help. Rest in his presence and come alive in his love today.

Jesus, you are my oasis of peace. I won't stop coming to you, nor will I stop bringing my burdens. You are greater than all of them. You are my peace. Fill me with the comfort of your presence and revive my weary heart.

REST IN HIS WISDOM

"Take my yoke upon you. Let me teach you,
because I am humble and gentle at heart,
and you will find rest for your souls."
MATTHEW 11:29 NLT

When we give God our heavy burdens, the next step is to learn from him. He is a gentle and humble teacher, and he leads us into rest. He does not overwhelm us with his knowledge, nor does he expect too much from us. He does not ridicule what we don't already know. He corrects us in kindness. In short, he's the best teacher there is.

The wisdom of God, as James 3:17 says, "is first of all pure. It is also peace-loving, gentle at all times, and willing to yield to others. It is full of mercy and the fruit of good deeds. It shows no favoritism and is always sincere." This is the wisdom Jesus teaches and embodies.

Wise One, I yield to your gentle wisdom that teaches me the best way to live. I follow you more than anyone else and rely on your truth to guide me through this life. My soul finds rest in you.

A LIGHTER LOAD

"The burden that I ask you to accept is easy;
the load I give you to carry is light."
MATTHEW 11:30 NCV

When Jesus asks us to partner with him, it doesn't mean
we get to opt out of our responsibilities or choices. The
load he asks us to carry, however, is light. It is not too
much. When we offer our heavy burdens to Jesus, he
willingly takes them. What he offers in return is easy
for us to bear.

After you lay down your burdens at Jesus' feet and receive
the rest and refreshment of his Spirit, he offers you
something to carry. What is the light load he offers you?
Is it to be kind to those who challenge you today? Is it to
refuse to fight with someone unwilling to listen to you?
Whatever it is, accept it with gratitude and joy today, for it
is much better than what you traded in.

Jesus, I will not neglect to accept what you offer
today. Thank you for the rest of your presence and the
refreshing peace of your tender care. I gladly take what
you give. Don't stop teaching me, Lord.

GOD'S CONCERNS

When Jesus turned and looked at his disciples, he rebuked
Peter. "Get behind me, Satan!" he said. "You do not have in
mind the concerns of God, but merely human concerns."

MARK 8:33 NIV

Peter loved Jesus. He didn't want to even entertain the
thought that Jesus might suffer. Peter tried to convince
Jesus to not talk in such sinister terms, but Jesus would
not be dissuaded. In fact, he rebuked Peter.

Have you tried to reduce someone's suffering—the
weight and power of it—by saying they should think
more positively? The thing is, suffering is part of life,
and avoiding discussions about it is not a holy act. Jesus
rebuked Peter for trying to keep him from speaking the
truth. The truth isn't always joyful, and we must learn to
accept that. Instead of dismissing others' pain, we must
make room for it, for God is concerned with our suffering
as much as our victories.

Jesus, thank you for setting the precedent for talking
about our pain. You didn't dismiss the suffering that was
coming, and you didn't hide it from your disciples. Teach
me to sit with the reality of suffering. Thank you for
being with me in my pain.

A NARROW PATH

"Make every effort to enter through the narrow door, because I tell you, many will try to enter and won't be able."
LUKE 13:24 CSB

There is a cost to enter the narrow door of God's kingdom. It is not easy to choose the pathway of God's love, for it requires dying to self. It requires continued humility. If we want to feast in the kingdom of heaven, we need to become like children, learning from Christ and putting aside what we thought we already knew from tradition.

If you humble yourself before God, let his guidance direct you, and stay softhearted in his love, he will lead you in the way of his everlasting life. Don't let swelling pride keep you from being small enough to enter. Lay down the things that keep you stuck and yield to Jesus' gentle leadership.

Lord, I don't want to waste my life for my own agenda. I want to live with your love as the primary banner over my life. I want to be known for that. Lead me through your narrow way and keep me on your path of life.

MORE IMPORTANT THINGS

"My food is to do the will of Him who sent Me,
and to finish His work."
JOHN 4:34 NKJV

The disciples were concerned that Jesus hadn't eaten anything. Jesus was focused, not on filling his belly, but on doing what God had sent him to do. Though the disciples meant well, Jesus was preoccupied with ministering to the people flocking to hear him speak.

Jesus could sense his time was limited. Don't we feel that when we're on a deadline? As Ecclesiastes says, there is a time to work and a time to rest. A time to sow and a time to reap. Jesus saw the harvest of people coming to him, and he knew it was time to work. May we also sense the spiritual seasons and give energy to what needs it in the moment. Sometimes, the most important thing to do is feed ourselves and rest; other times, it's serving those who come to us.

Jesus, thank you for being willing to do the will of the Father. Thank you for salvation, freedom, and your limitless love. I can never thank you enough.

MAY

"Love the Lord your God
with all your heart
and will all your soul
and with all your mind."

MATTHEW 22:37 NIV

RECOGNIZE THE WORK

"I sent you to reap that for which you have not labored;
others have labored, and you have come into their labor."
JOHN 4:38 NASB

How often do we recognize those who have gone before
us and laid the foundation for the lives we now live? Our
actions have consequences that are good, neutral, or bad.
The focus of our lives, what we build, is left to those who
come after us. If we see past our little parts, we can impact
generational legacies.

When we enter seasons of plenty, it's often not our work
that got us there. Jesus said he was sending his disciples
to reap a harvest they had not sown. This is true of us
as well. Through the lens of gratitude, we recognize
how interconnected we are while we play our parts. We
resist the pull of pride that fools us into thinking all we
accomplish is our doing. In reality, it's a partnership of
others' sacrifices as well as our own.

Jesus, I don't want to be arrogant or ignorant about
my successes. There is more at work, more labor and
sacrifice at the foundation, than I am able to see. I
honor what others have done, and I join in the great
partnership of faith.

COMFORT IN GRIEF

"Blessed are those who mourn,
for they shall be comforted."
Matthew 5:4 esv

All who grieve will be comforted. Isaiah 61 declares what Jesus came to do: "to bind up the brokenhearted…to comfort all who mourn; to give them…the oil of gladness instead of mourning, the garment of praise instead of a faint spirit" (vs. 1-3). This is his promise to us. The Spirit of the Lord does this, and we know that the Spirit is already with us.

The perfection of relief will come when Jesus restores the earth, but until then, we have the presence of his Spirit to minister comfort and relief. He gives us beauty for our ashes and the oil of gladness for our mourning. We don't need to resist his peace. It is persistent even, and especially, in our greatest pain.

Comforter, I rely on you not only when things go well but also when everything falls apart. Be near in comfort and fill me with your peace. Wrap me in your embrace even when I can't look up. Minister to me in my pain and wash me in your love.

GREATEST COMMANDMENT

"You are to love the Lord Yahweh, your God, with every passion of your heart, with all the energy of your being, with every thought that is within you, and with all your strength. This is the great and supreme commandment."

MARK 12:30 TPT

The greatest commandment is not an invitation to rigidity but to devotion. As we love the Lord with the passion of our hearts, the energy of our being, the thoughts within us, and every bit of strength, it becomes the core of our why. Why are we kind to others? Because we love the Lord. Why extend grace when others would ridicule or dismiss? Because of our love for God.

Is love the driving force of your faith? If not, take some time to connect to God through his Spirit. We love because God first loved us. No matter how lacking we are in any moment, we need only receive the abundant love that Christ offers us first. When we are filled with his love, it will overflow from us.

Christ, I can't perfectly love you, but I choose to love you nonetheless. Thank you for not requiring perfection but devotion. May my heart, thoughts, and actions reflect the passion of your love in my life.

HONEST AND OPEN

"The seeds that fell on the good soil represent honest, good-hearted people who hear God's word, cling to it, and patiently produce a huge harvest."

LUKE 8:15 NLT

Loving and following God requires perseverance. If we continue to surrender to his correction, do what he asks, and live out his love, we will grow and mature until our lives produce the fruit of his Spirit at work within us.

No matter what we do, the fruit of those things will be evident. If we want the fruit of the kingdom of God to grow in us, then we need to be honest with ourselves and others and live with integrity. When we hear the word of the Lord, take it to heart, and put it into practice, a crop of righteousness will come. Let's not give up.

Lord, I don't want to fool myself with pride or think I know better than you do. I trust you, and even when I have to wait on your timing, I choose to follow you. I trust you are at work in every stage and in every step along my journey.

NOTHING IS IMPOSSIBLE

"With people it is impossible, but not with God—
God makes all things possible!"
MARK 10:27 TPT

For today's verse, the context of Jesus' statement is illuminating. "God makes all things possible" is true regardless, but when we discover Jesus was talking about how people might be saved and enter into God's kingdom realm, we can appreciate that we don't enter by our own strength. It is through Christ alone because God made this possible.

This is liberating news! We don't have to be perfect. In fact, God knew perfection was always out of our reach. That's why he sent Christ to become our perfection. Christ is our covering, and we enter God's kingdom through him. No matter who we are, what we've done, or where we come from, this is true. "With people it is impossible, but not with God." Hallelujah!

Savior, I am humbled once again at the beauty, power, and specificity of your sacrifice. Thank you for saving us. You knew we could never do it on our own. I will not resist you, Lord. You are life, hope, and joy to me.

SAME LOVE

"This is my command:
Love each other as I have loved you."
JOHN 15:12 NCV

To love others as Jesus has loved us is a high, high bar. Though no one is perfect in love, we have been perfected in Christ's love. It should be our goal to love with the same abandon that Jesus did.

Our excuses as to why we should not serve certain people, show compassion to the suffering, or promote peace where others incite violence fall flat in the light of this command. How Jesus loved his followers, how he loves us, and how he loves the world: this is how we are to love each other. With this in mind, our choices become clear. No expectation of us matters more than Christ's does.

Jesus, I have no excuses today. I bring my regret, my ideas, and my heart, and I surrender them all to you. May I choose to walk in your love even, and especially, when it's hard.

SINCERE TRUST

"Don't be like them, because your Father knows
the things you need before you ask him."
MATTHEW 6:8 CSB

Instead of repeating empty phrases as we pray, hoping
that God will hear us, Jesus assures us the Father already
knows our needs before we ask him. If we want to connect
to God in prayer and not just talk at him, we can use the
example Jesus gave us.

As we pray to the Father, we center ourselves around the
glory of his being. We ask him to manifest his kingdom
realm on the earth and fulfill his purposes here as he does
in heaven. We acknowledge God as our provider. We ask
for forgiveness, and we commit to forgiving others in the
same way. We ask for the Lord's help in every test and ask
him to set us free from evil. We proclaim as the King who
rules over all and give him the glory. This prayer builds
trust in our hearts as we connect to the one who is greater
than anything we face.

Lord, I long to connect heart-to-heart, spirit-to-Spirit, as
I pray today. Meet me as I turn my attention toward you.
You are my help, and you are powerful to save. Thank you.

MORE THAN A GLIMPSE

When Jesus reached the spot, he looked up
and said to him, "Zacchaeus, come down immediately.
I must stay at your house today."
LUKE 19:5 NIV

Zacchaeus was a short man, and he wanted to see Jesus
through the crowd. He did what made sense to him; he
climbed a tree to get a glimpse of Jesus. Seeing him in the
tree, Jesus told him to come down because he would eat
at his house that day. Jesus saw the eagerness in the man,
and although he was a tax collector with a bad reputation,
it did not deter him from going to his home.

We can't keep Jesus away when he sets his mind on us.
God's purposes are for all who seek him to find him.
Thieves and liars will find peace in the presence of Christ
as they submit to his ways. Let's not disqualify ourselves,
nor anyone else for that matter, from following Christ. His
love does not discriminate, and neither should we.

Jesus, I love that you did not care about whom you
offended with your generosity. I don't want to be
offended by you, Lord. I remain open and eager to
catch a glimpse of you no matter who it's through.

BELIEF AND TRUST

"Whatever things you ask when you pray,
believe that you receive them, and you will have them."
MARK 11:24 NKJV

Do we believe God is who he says he is? Do we trust he
is faithful, powerful, and able to do more than we can
imagine? Then let's take him at his word. When we pray,
let's believe that God not only hears us but that he'll
answer.

Jesus was not afraid to pray about what was on his heart.
Remember the prayer he prayed in Gethsemane? He
asked that the Lord take away his need to suffer. There is a
divine difference here, though; he already knew he must
do it. In the end, he yielded to God's will. We also can pray
believing that God hears and answers. Let's also yield to
the Lord's will when we can't escape what is coming. In the
tension of both/and, we will find where that trust dwells.

Jesus, I believe I will walk in the power of your Spirit and
move in the might of your miracles. I also know there
are certain things I can't escape. Help me to know the
difference and trust you regardless.

NO ONE TO BLAME

"It was neither that this man sinned, nor his parents; but it was so that the works of God might be displayed in him."
JOHN 9:3 NASB

How often do we judge others by their circumstances? Sickness is not a punishment, and mental health struggles are not a formal accusation of sin. We live in a world where a myriad of factors affects our environments and our bodies. It's not helpful to shame, blame, or offer unwanted opinions on those dealing with tough issues.

God's mighty power is ready to meet us wherever we struggle. God didn't intend for us to get stuck in cycles that keep us from living in the freedom of his purposes for us. We can yield to his love and invite his mercy to empower, heal, and liberate us. His love casts no shadow of shame. With that in mind, clothing ourselves in his compassion, we can follow wherever he leads.

Liberator, I partner with your heart today. When I come up with reasons why someone is suffering, may I humble my heart in your wise love. There is no need to cast blame; you are the one who sets us free.

WHERE THE HEART IS

"Well did Isaiah prophesy of you hypocrites, as it is written,
'This people honors Me with their lips,
But their heart is far from Me."
MARK 7:6 NKJV

It does not matter how religious a person appears to be; the posture of their heart is what matters. 1 Samuel 16:7 says, "Man looks on the outward appearance, but the Lord looks on the heart." It doesn't matter how strong, pure, or put-together we seem if our hearts are not yielded to the Lord in humble love.

No one can know the heart of a person other than the one who holds it and the one who made it. We should not be impressed or intimidated by those who seem to have it all together. No one is perfect. No one escapes suffering. No one is without temptation. Guard your heart, stay humble, and allow the Lord to mold you with his mercy.

Lord, thank you for the reminder that there is no perfect person. I don't want to waste my time comparing my life to others who seem more qualified. You are the ultimate qualifier, and you look at the heart rather than the shell. I yield to you.

PURSUING WHAT MATTERS

"Your heart will always pursue
what you value as your treasure."
MATTHEW 6:21 TPT

Our hearts go after what we value. We pursue what we find most precious. What desires fill your mind? What do you give your time, resources, and service to?

It is never too late to change course. If we discover that the things we treasured aren't actually the most valuable, we can adjust. This is where our choices partner with the grace of God to shift our trajectory. We can start with what we fill our minds with and what we allow to take up emotional and mental energy. Our lives reflect our values, so we must not overlook the importance of intention when coupled with consistent practice.

Jesus, I want my heart to pursue the things on your heart. This will come through fellowship and submission to you. Transform my heart in yours, Lord.

STRENGTH OF FORGIVENESS

"Even if that person wrongs you seven times a day and each time turns again and asks forgiveness, you must forgive."
LUKE 17:4 NLT

No matter how many times we are wronged, we should be willing to forgive. We do this as much for ourselves as we do for those we forgive. Where unforgiveness resides, the root of bitterness grows. It erodes our peace.

Forgiveness isn't weak. It takes a strong person to forgive over and over. Jesus did not tell his disciples they should forgive their brother seven times a day so they could stop forgiving at the eighth time. No, he meant there should be no limit to our forgiveness. It takes grace, humility, strength, and courage to choose to forgive. May we be people of such graceful strength.

Jesus, you forgive more than any of us. As God, you have been sinned against and hurt more than any other being. I trust your wisdom has purpose. Give me strength and courage to forgive others as you forgive me freely each time I come to you.

OUR GREATEST HELPER

"The Helper will teach you everything and will cause you to remember all that I told you. This Helper is the Holy Spirit whom the Father will send in my name."
JOHN 14:26 NCV

The Holy Spirit is our helper, not only in chaos and confusion, but whenever we need him. He instructs us and reminds us of the words of Christ. He knows exactly what we need, and what we need to hear, in every moment.

When we cultivate a relationship with the Holy Spirit and honor him as we do Christ and the Father, we honor God. The Spirit is part of the Triune God and as powerful as God's other persons. He moves with mighty mercy through the earth. At the same time, the Spirit makes his home in us. His presence can't be contained, and he can't be controlled. He helps those who trust him rather than themselves.

Helper, thank you for your presence in my life. Teach me and speak to me; I am listening. I long for a refreshing word spoken at the right time. You know what I need, Spirit.

COURAGE TO CONTINUE

The following night, the Lord stood by him and said, "Have courage! For as you have testified about me in Jerusalem, so it is necessary for you to testify in Rome."
ACTS 23:11 CSB

Paul's testimony before the priests and religious council was not easy. He faced an intense barrage of threats and questions. He did not back down but stood on the truth revealed to him by Christ. He must have been tired. He barely escaped with his life!

Jesus appeared to him and told him to keep his courage up. He said Paul would also testify in Rome. It took a tremendous amount of bravery for Paul to go from one council to the next knowing that others vehemently disagreed with him. Still, Paul counted himself as already crucified with Christ: "It is no longer I who live, but it is Christ who lives in me" (Galatians 2:20). May we have the courage to face whatever Christ calls us to do. We have the help of the Spirit of Christ through it all.

Christ Jesus, live in me. Embolden and awaken my heart in strength and faith. I am yours, and I will not back down from where you lead me.

HOPE OF GLORY

"Whoever has ears, let them hear what the Spirit says
to the churches. To the one who is victorious,
I will give some of the hidden manna. I will also
give that person a white stone with a new name written
on it, known only to the one who receives it."

REVELATION 2:17 NIV

Fellowship of the Spirit reveals mysteries; God whispers secrets to each of us. As devoted lovers of Christ, we find our treasure in the give-and-take relationship the Spirit of God offers. There is abounding hope in the living relationship we have with God.

We must open our ears to hear what the Spirit has to say, not only to us personally, but to his church as a whole. Christ's victory is our victory; he gives us the strength to persevere through every trial we face. We never go it alone. There is sufficient provision, and there are endless revelations of God's mysteries if we keep going after him.

Victorious One, may your triumph be my own. I want to know you more than I have up to this point. Draw me deeper into your wisdom with your love. I won't stop pursuing you.

BLESS NOT CURSE

*"Love your enemies, bless those who curse you,
do good to those who hate you, and pray for those
who spitefully use you and persecute you."*
MATTHEW 5:44 NKJV

How we treat each other matters more than our religious rituals. If we go to church every Sunday yet curse those who badmouth us, we are not walking in the love of the Lord. Jesus said his disciples would be known by their love. If we are not known by our extravagant love, then we have some reprioritizing to do.

Generous love does not keep a record of wrongs. It does not return evil for evil, and it does not curse those who hurt. It always chooses the better and right way. Love expands while fear restricts. Are we living in the liberty of Christ's love, or are we living in fear of others' expectations? As we bless those who curse us, do good to those who despise us, and pray for those who persecute us, we reflect the Lord's love.

Jesus, your ways are better than the world's ways, but I need your grace and power to walk in them. Help me choose your ways.

MORE THAN WORDS

He took them in His arms and began blessing them,
laying His hands on them.
MARK 10:16 NASB

Jesus poured a beautiful display of affection over the
children who came to him. He welcomed them with open
arms and blessed each one. Not only did Jesus tell his
disciples to let children come to him, but he treated them
as people and not lesser beings. Jesus dignified these
children by meeting them on their level.

He still never turns away a curious and hungry child. May
our inner children lead us to Jesus. There, he welcomes
us with an embrace and blesses us with the touch of his
presence. An incredible exchange awaits us; let's not delay
a moment longer.

Compassionate One, your love is better than any I've
known. You don't put limits on whom you welcome, and
you embrace all who come to you with an open heart.
Here I am, Lord; take me in your arms. Love me to life in
your presence and speak your words of wisdom over me.

ANSWERS TO LIFE

"You shall love the Lord your God with all your heart and with all your soul and with all your strength and with all your mind, and your neighbor as yourself."
LUKE 10:27 ESV

We already know to love the Lord our God with all heart, soul, strength, and mind. But what about the second part of today's Scripture? Do we love our neighbors as we do ourselves? Do we consider their preferences, boundaries, and needs as much as our own?

Loving God can feel ideological when he isn't in front of us. When we are called to love our neighbor—our nosy, loud, or disagreeable neighbor—what then? They have faces, names, and temperaments. We must not over-spiritualize our faith and forget that love looks like kindness and generosity.

Jesus, help me love my neighbor the way I want to be treated. Grow my spirit with practical acts of kindness, generosity, and care even when a thank you never comes. Your love is my example.

PERFECT PEACE

"I leave the gift of peace with you—my peace. Not the kind of fragile peace given by the world, but my perfect peace. Don't yield to fear or be troubled in your hearts—instead, be courageous!"
JOHN 14:27 TPT

The peace of Christ surpasses our understanding; it is greater than our best attempt at imagining it. Paul said it this way in Philippians: "God's wonderful peace that transcends human understanding, will make the answers known to you through Jesus Christ" (4:7). When we tell God every detail of our lives and give him our worries, his peace fills the empty space.

Don't yield to fear. Jesus promises he is with you through his Spirit; his Word says it over and over. He is with you every day. He has given you himself, his very presence, as your peace. What a wonderful gift.

Peace-Giver, your presence is my life, breath, and hope. You are my strength and courage. It is always you. Thank you for the gracious gift of yourself.

SALT OF WISDOM

"You are the salt of the earth. But what good is salt if it has lost its flavor? Can you make it salty again? It will be thrown out and trampled underfoot as worthless."
MATTHEW 5:13 NLT

Salt is used as a seasoning to enhance the flavors of many dishes. When Jesus calls us the "salt of the earth," he means our lives should make the world, and the people around us, better. If we lose our potency and purpose, what use do we have?

Jesus calls us to reflect his love, kingdom, and peace in the earth. We are filled with these things ourselves to then share with others. We can look to Jesus, our Redeemer, and allow him to transform us in his image. As we soak up the nutrients of his kingdom, we have more to offer others.

Jesus, I don't want to waste my life letting foolish distractions, arguments, or mandatory isolation keep me from sharing what you freely offer. May my life enhance what you have already begun in those around me.

FAITH CONQUERS FEAR

Jesus paid no attention to what they said. He told the
synagogue leader, "Don't be afraid; just believe."
MARK 5:36 NCV

There will always be opinions that say we should be
skeptical about something or other. When Jesus speaks
to us, encouraging us to not be afraid but to believe
that what he said is true, he calls our minds and hearts
into focus. His Word is our anchor. His redemptive and
restorative power is our tuning fork.

In a world filled with naysayers, don't let what others
say deter you from believing what Jesus speaks. He is
unfailing in love, and he is faithful to each of his promises.
When he tells you to take courage and not yield to fear,
it is because he is with you, and he knows what deserves
your mental and emotional energy. His love conquers fear
every time. "Don't be afraid; just believe."

Jesus, I trust your Word more than I trust those who
doubt it. You are living and active in the world around
me and in my life. My faith is in you, and you are my
focal point and anchor.

CHOOSE YOUR PATH

"No servant can serve two masters, since either he will hate
one and love the other, or he will be devoted to one and
despise the other. You cannot serve both God and money."
LUKE 16:13 CSB

God's concerns are more diverse than our bank accounts
and comfort. Serving his interests means laying down
our self-promoting tendencies and partnering with his
generosity. It looks like surrendering even when others
would call it foolish. When we are more concerned with
wealth than with spiritual submission, we will always
choose what serves us over what could benefit our
communities or the kingdom of God.

This doesn't mean money is the enemy. It is a tool.
However, love of money and the pursuit of wealth can
consume us if we are not careful. We can't choose to
surrender fully to God if we are focused on becoming
rich. They are two different focuses that will call for
vastly different choices. We must choose which is more
important to us.

Jesus, I don't want to be consumed with my own
comfort or what benefits me more than the greater
good of humanity. May I walk this path you have laid
out. Your ways are better than any I could plan myself,
and I trust you.

NOT BY SIGHT

"Because you have seen me, you have believed; blessed
are those who have not seen and yet have believed."
JOHN 20:29 NIV

The disciples, the many people Jesus ministered to, as well
as family and friends, got to experience the glory of the
Son of God in person. Even so, he was inescapably human.
He was a man. From birth to adulthood, he grew, went
through puberty, and learned just as we all do. Still, who
could deny the power of God moving through his mighty
miracles of mercy?

Jesus was patient with Thomas even in his doubt. He
revealed himself to Thomas and allowed him to touch the
wounds which were still present in his resurrected body.
Jesus did not turn him away. Jesus also blessed those in
the future who would believe without seeing. That's us! As
Paul said, we live by faith and not sight. We have not seen
Jesus in the flesh, yet we believe. We are mightily blessed.

Lord Jesus, thank you for your Spirit who fills my being
with your presence. You are still moving today just as
you did when you walked the earth. You are the Son of
God and my Savior.

CONFESSIONS OF FAITH

"Whoever confesses Me before men, him the Son of Man also will confess before the angels of God."
LUKE 12:8 NKJV

Jesus Christ, the Son of God, came to seek and to save the lost, the downhearted and down-on-their luck, the hopeless, and the abandoned. He came to offer the abundant life of God's kingdom to every person who receives him. There is no reason to be ashamed of him. He is not ashamed of any of us.

If we claim to live for Christ but hesitate to share the power of his love at work in us, what are we hiding? We don't have to align with any system on this earth to align with Jesus. He is above it all. Where others seek to contain him, he can't be pinned down. Is our shame based on who he is? Or are we ashamed of what others might assume? The truth of Christ is much more redemptive than our earthly affiliations. Let's look to him and give him the glory he's due.

Jesus, I am not ashamed to be known as yours, for you are the way, the truth, and my liberating life.

MOVING MOUNTAINS

"Truly I say to you, whoever says to this mountain,
'Be taken up and thrown into the sea,' and does not doubt
in his heart, but believes that what he says is going to
happen, it will be granted to him."

MARK 11:23 NASB

There is active power in faith. God gives us the gift of faith;
it is not something we stir up on our own. As we get to
know God's faithfulness, our trust in his present power
grows. We learn he is always loyal to his Word, and he
will not fail.

We have an incredible invitation to partner with what
God is already doing and carry the power and authority
of Christ. When Jesus commissioned his disciples to
go and minister, he said, "Heal the sick, raise the dead,
cleanse those with leprosy, cast out demons. Freely you
have received; freely give" (Matthew 10:8). This is our
commissioning as well.

Mountain Mover, you are full of power, and you freely
share it with your people. I want to walk in your
authority with your compassion driving me to do what
you told your disciples to do. Increase my faith.

NO NEED TO FLAUNT

"That your fasting may not be seen by others but by your Father who is in secret. And your Father who sees in secret will reward you."
MATTHEW 6:18 ESV

In Jesus' day, those who fasted for religious reasons would often be obvious about it. Their show of suffering was to prove how holy they were. Jesus said when we fast, however, we should not let on to others that we are doing it. Fasting is personal, and it pleases God when we keep it between him and us.

This same principle goes for any of the spiritual disciplines. When we pray, we do it not for the audience of others but for God. Especially spiritually, we have no reason to show off. God is not impressed by what may or may not impress others. Stay honest, humble, true, and open. We don't owe anyone but God the surrender of our hearts; we have nothing to prove.

Lord, thank you for taking the pressure off when it comes to fasting and prayer. It is not for others to see and know but for you alone. I trust you know my heart and will honor my intentions.

YOUR DESTINY

"Get up and stand to your feet, for I have appeared to
you to reveal your destiny and to commission you as my
assistant. You will be a witness to what you have seen and
to the things I will reveal whenever I appear to you."
ACTS 26:16 TPT

Every person is called by God. When we answer his call,
he reveals our destiny and commissions us to partner
with his purposes. Our destinies are as vast as our unique
personalities and perfectly suited to us. What your friend
has been called to is their own, and your calling may be
completely different. The important task isn't figuring
it out; it's developing a relationship with the one who
created you.

Through fellowship, the Lord will reveal to you your
unique partnership with his purposes. It may look nothing
like you expect, but as you serve with an open and willing
heart, he will use you. Don't go searching the earth for
your purpose. There's no need. Do what is yours to do now
and submit to the Lord as he reveals each new step.

Holder of my destiny, I trust your redemptive power is
at work in my life. I want to know your voice's tone and
timbre as clearly as I know my own. I am yours, Lord.

EXTRAVAGANT WORSHIP

"Leave her alone.
She did this in preparation for my burial."
JOHN 12:7 NLT

In his religious mindset, Judas questioned the seeming waste of expensive perfume as Mary poured it over Jesus' feet and anointed him with it. He thought it would have been better to have sold the perfume and donated the money to the poor. What was wasted in his mind, however, was a meaningful act of loving worship to Jesus.

Jesus often came to the defense of those others ridiculed. Mary loved Jesus, and Jesus honored that. We need never fear Jesus' response to our worship. He honors every sacrifice we make. Even when others do not understand, Jesus does. May that be enough.

Lord Jesus, I pour my love on you. You are worthy of my time, attention, costly resources, and more. You are worthy of it all. I won't let what others think keep me from worshiping you, for I know you see me. You know my heart, and you will honor what is offered in love.

LIVING SOMEONE'S DREAM

"I tell you the truth, many prophets and good people wanted to see the things that you now see, but they did not see them. And they wanted to hear the things that you now hear, but they did not hear them."

MATTHEW 13:17 NCV

No matter who we are, where we are, or what we do, there is something good in our lives that someone else longs for. This was true of the disciples in Jesus' day; they got to live and interact with the Word made flesh. It's true for us as well. We may miss the blessing in front of us, however, if we are preoccupied with what we don't have.

Instead of comparing our dreams with the lives of others, gratitude cultivates its power in the present and what is already ours. Spiritually and physically, we have more than we often recognize. We can dig deep wells of appreciation that bring life and refreshment to every part of life. With our eyes focused on the goodness of God, we can celebrate our gifts.

Jesus, give me eyes to see all the blessings already present in my life. I want to overflow with gratitude and not endlessly grasp for what is out of reach. You are with me, and that is more than enough.

PRACTICAL GOODNESS

He took her by the hand and said to her, "Talitha koum!"
(which means "Little girl, I say to you, get up!")
MARK 5:41 NIV

After he raised this young child from the dead, Jesus told her parents to give her something to eat. While we may not know the significance of this, Jesus was concerned and cared for the both the girl's body and soul. He brought her back to life, and he knew exactly what she needed.

This is still true today. When God calls us out of the realm of the dead into the living, he also provides for our physical needs. We are not to ignore the commonsense practices that nourish our bodies, souls, and minds. Jesus always knows what to do, and sometimes, his advice is just practical. Don't ignore the simplicity and practicality of God's Word in your life.

Jesus, thank you for caring for not just our souls but our bodies as well. Your truth is grounded in reality, yet it supersedes my understanding of it. Speak to me, and I will do as you say. I am listening.

JUNE

"Even the Son of Man
did not come to be served,
but to serve,
and to give his life
as a ransom for many."

MARK 10:45 NIV

SEEDS OF FAITH

"If you have faith the size of a mustard seed," the Lord said, "you can say to this mulberry tree, 'Be uprooted and planted in the sea,' and it will obey you."

Luke 17:6 csb

With small seeds of faith come many, many possibilities. Jesus is more gracious with us than we give him credit for. He is not a cruel overseer, and he patiently teaches us as we partner with him.

Faith grows in the soil of God's loyal love. We don't have to strive to grow in faith. As we fellowship with Jesus and know him more, our trust in his faithfulness grows. His ways become our ways; his thoughts become our thoughts. His confidence and authority become the nutrient-dense food for our faith. Only in him and through him do we find ourselves with the smallest seeds of conviction.

Lord Jesus, as I grow closer to you, increase my assurance in your faithfulness. Your nature never changes. You are always good, true, and merciful. Your power knows no limits. Please nurture my small seed of faith.

ABIDING POWER

"If you abide in Me, and My words abide in you, you will ask what you desire, and it shall be done for you."
JOHN 15:7 NKJV

As we dwell in the vine of Jesus, we are connected to the source of his wisdom. We can't be entwined with him and not benefit from the nourishment he offers. He is the vine, and we are his branches. When our lives produce the fruit of his Spirit, we demonstrate we are his mature disciples. Why? Only mature trees are fruit-bearing.

Whatever season we find ourselves in, whether a dormant one or a fruit-bearing one, we can be confident that the life of Jesus gives us all we need when we remain connected to him. This is the power of abiding. His Spirit runs through us and provides nourishment straight from the source. If we do nothing else today, let's abide in him.

Jesus, I am yours. I never want to be disconnected from your powerful presence. Even when my life doesn't look abundant, you provide all I need. I trust you. I abide in you.

GOD OF THE LIVING

"He is not the God of the dead, but of the living;
you are greatly mistaken."
MARK 12:27 NASB

When we value a person no longer alive more than the people in front of us, we miss the powerful mercy of Christ available now. This goes for historical figures as well as personal ones. If we revere the memory of someone but do not allow their faults to exist, we idolize them instead of honoring them.

God's mercy is living and active. It is concerned with those who need it now. His compassion is powerful enough to cover both the dead and the living, but we shouldn't get caught up in defending or arguing a case for those who have passed when someone right in front of us is asking us to understand their struggle. Let's not put off extending God's mercy to anyone.

Jesus, you are alive, and your power reaches everyone, everywhere. Keep me from getting caught up in issues that separate thought from action and dehumanize those asking for justice and mercy. You never withhold it; may I do as you do.

ALREADY COVERED

"Therefore I tell you, do not be anxious about your life,
what you will eat or what you will drink, nor about your
body, what you will put on. Is not life more than food,
and the body more than clothing?"
MATTHEW 6:25 ESV

When Jesus asks us to trust him, he asks not just for our
spirits and souls but for our very bodies. God is a good
father. He provides all we need. When God calls us to
follow him, he promises to satisfy our needs. Instead of
getting caught up in the anxieties of the unknown, we can
rest in the faithfulness of God.

Philippians 4:6-7 says it well: "Do not be anxious about
anything, but in everything by prayer and supplication
with thanksgiving let your requests be made known
to God. And the peace of God, which surpasses all
understanding, will guard your hearts and minds in Christ
Jesus." Perhaps it's time to share some anxieties with your
Lord in prayer today.

All-Knowing One, I trust your provision in my life. You
always take care of me, so I will not worry about what is
coming. I give you my anxiety and turn my heart to you.

WORTH IT

"The kingdom of heaven is like a merchant looking for fine pearls. When he found one of great value, he went away and sold everything he had and bought it."
MATTHEW 13:45-46 NIV

Throughout the gospels, Jesus compares the kingdom of heaven to many things. In this case, he says it is like a merchant who, upon finding a valuable pearl, sells everything he has to buy it. We are not the merchant; Jesus is. We are the unique pearl Jesus sees as extremely valuable and worth giving his life for.

Jesus, even knowing our flaws and weaknesses, sees us as valuable. He wants us as his own. He wanted it so much, in fact, that he was willing to give up all he had in exchange for us. What kind of love is this? It's stronger than our wavering passions. It's stronger than the grave itself. Knowing that Jesus sees you as worthy of his sacrifice, are you willing to offer him anything in return?

Jesus, I can't comprehend the depths of your love. Show me what you see in me. I want to walk in the confidence of your love.

WHEN YOU FALTER

"Betrayals are inevitable, but great devastation will come to the one guilty of betraying others."

LUKE 17:1 TPT

There is a difference between faltering in your step and leading someone down a path riddled with obstacles. Though Jesus says we should expect betrayals in life, we should be careful not to be the one who betrays others.

He goes on to say it would be better to be buried at sea, hurled into the waters with a heavy boulder tied around the neck, than to betray one of his dear ones. Jesus wants us to treat others with love at all times. There will be people who work to make others stumble, and that is never a loving act. Jesus picks up those who falter and leads them back to his path because he is kind and trustworthy.

Jesus, your love does not condone bad behavior, yet you offer so much grace to us. I can't thank you enough. Keep my feet on your path.

FOOD IS FOOD

"Food doesn't go into your heart,
but only passes through the stomach and then goes
into the sewer." [By saying this, he declared that every
kind of food is acceptable in God's eyes.]

MARK 7:19 NLT

Jesus took the morality out of food when he told his followers that what you eat or don't eat doesn't make you holy or unclean; what is in the heart does. Up until this point, the law of Moses had strict rules about food. Jesus, however, set the record straight. He changed the standard. Holiness isn't about what we eat or drink; it's about the content of our hearts.

It isn't hard to imagine what food morality looks like; it's all around us. From clean eating to the newest trendy diet, people use food to project an image of inner goodness. We know this isn't true. What passes through our digestive system doesn't make us righteous, good, or moral. It's what goes into, and flows from, our hearts.

Jesus, I don't want to get caught up in thinking I'm less than or better than anyone else based on what I eat. Thank you for your truth and loving perspective.

WORSHIP JESUS

"It is written in the Scriptures: 'You must worship the Lord
your God and serve only him.'"
LUKE 4:8 NCV

When Jesus was tempted in the desert, one of the enemy's major appeals was an offer of power over all the kingdoms and regions of the world. All Jesus had to do was bow down and worship him. In Jesus' response today, we see the simplicity of God's command and how Jesus knew the Word well enough to stand upon it.

Temptation is not easy to overcome, but when we are rooted and grounded in God's Word, we can combat it with the sword of his authority. We worship the Lord our God and only bow down to him. Jesus, as Messiah and Son of God, is worthy of our worship. He also is acquainted with temptation. Use his triumph as proof that you can also overcome. He is your strength and deliverer.

Jesus, thank you for the boldness and strength you showed through your submission to the Father and to his Word. When temptation is pulling me, bring your Word to mind and give me grace and strength to stand upon it.

DON'T JUDGE

"Do not judge, so that you won't be judged."
MATTHEW 7:1 CSB

When we are full of criticism for others, we will receive that same standard in return. If we hold others to a greater standard than we hold ourselves to, we lose the grounding grace our lives are built on. We are no better than anyone else. Truly.

There is a difference between accountability and judgment. The former appeals to the person and offers an opportunity for restoration, repentance, and redemption. The latter does not engage with the offender at all. It builds a foundation full of holes, like a net, to capture others in their sin. The trick is that the net is hidden in the soil of our hearts and can trap us too. Let's be merciful and gracious instead and offer others the benefit of the doubt until we know that confrontation and accountability are needed.

Jesus, where I err toward criticism and judgment, I yield to your love. I don't want to be known as an unrelenting critic. I want to be known for the mercy and grace I give even while standing for justice. Thank you for your help in this.

ENDLESS OPPORTUNITIES

"The poor you have with you always,
but Me you do not have always."
JOHN 12:8 NKJV

This verse was a direct reply to Judas who was criticizing Mary for wasting expensive perfume by pouring it out over Jesus' feet. He thought it should have been sold and the proceeds given to the poor instead. Jesus thought differently. Why?

There is a time for everything. There is time to worship the Lord in extravagant ways and time to get in the dirt and help the poor. They can be one and the same. The thing is, we can't give to everyone in need. We don't have individual responsibility to meet every need presented to us. Does this mean we give up and don't try? Not at all! We partner with Christ in generously giving our money when we are able. In the same week, we can worship the Lord by using our time to praise him. It all matters.

Jesus, I need your wisdom and grace to properly use my time and resources. Show me where I am needed. Help me let go of the responsibility of meeting every need presented to me. Free me from that guilt in your love.

KNOCK

"Ask and it will be given to you; seek and you will find;
knock and the door will be opened to you."

MATTHEW 7:7 NIV

Whatever you are looking for, you will find. What you set your heart on, you will seek out. This is the way of things. What better pursuit than the pursuit of God's kingdom? Christ is full of truth, and he offers his wisdom to all who knock on the door of his kingdom through prayer.

Let this be the encouragement you need to keep seeking. There are times when rest is necessary. Whatever you do, don't close off your heart from Christ. Even when you are weary, he meets you where you are when you call. Ask, seek, and knock.

Jesus Christ, no one in heaven or on earth compares to you. Thank you for welcoming me with all my questions, longings, and flaws. I knock on the door of your presence today. Fill me with goodness, wisdom, and all I need.

FOR A GOAL

"Do not hinder him, for there is no one who will perform a miracle in My name, and be able soon afterward to speak evil of Me. For the one who is not against us is for us."
MARK 9:39-40 NASB

Nobody who performs miracles in the name of Jesus is covertly working for the enemy. Jesus set this straight when his disciples mentioned they had tried to stop someone, who wasn't a part of their group, from using Jesus' name to cast out demons. Instead of praising his disciples, he corrected them.

How often are we quick to judge those who don't meet the standards we feel are necessary to follow Jesus? How about to minister on his behalf? The truth is what Jesus said to his disciples: "The one who is not against us is for us." Don't try to stop those who are living, ministering, and loving others in the name of Christ.

Lord, keep my heart humble in your love and free from judgment. Your kingdom is not an exclusive club; it's an inclusive family full of people different from me. Thank you for making me part of your family.

ROOM FOR GRACE

Jesus turned and scolded them. [And Jesus said, "You don't know what kind of spirit you belong to. The Son of Man did not come to destroy the souls of people but to save them."] Then they went to another town.

LUKE 9:55-56 NCV

When Jesus was rejected from entering a Samaritan village, the disciples, instead of accepting it, wanted Jesus to call down fire from heaven and destroy them. Though it sounds drastic to us, this was the understanding of God through the Old Testament lens. Elijah had done just that with one such village.

Jesus did not agree. He rebuked his disciples and their hard-heartedness. Jesus came to bring life and set people free rather than condemn or destroy them. Jesus consistently revealed the Father as a God of mercy. There is always room for more grace. We can live with generosity even when others are not receptive.

Son of Man, I love your heart of mercy. Help me love in the same generous manner you did. I don't want to destroy others' lives—especially not in your name.

CONNECTION WITH CHRIST

When Jesus saw him lying there, he knew that the man
had been crippled for a long time. So Jesus said to him,
"Do you truly long to be healed?"

JOHN 5:6 TPT

Even though Jesus knew the man he approached had
been crippled for a long time, he reached out to connect
before doing anything further. Jesus could have healed
him in a moment without a conversation, but he asked,
"Do you truly long to be healed?"

This man was sitting at the edge of a pool that was known
to have healing effects. Yes, he wanted to be healed!
Jesus, gracious and kind, did not rebuke this man for his
response; rather, he told him to stand up and pick up his
mat. The man did so, and he was healed. Jesus is not just
a healer; he is a friend. Lean into the connection he offers
and then follow his directions.

Christ Jesus, I am humbled to be known by you. You
already know everything about me, but you draw me
into connection through your Spirit. Speak, Lord,
and I will answer you. Lead, and I will follow.

AT A LOSS

"I asked, 'What should I do, Lord?'
And the Lord told me, 'Get up and go into Damascus,
and there you will be told everything you are to do.'"
ACTS 22:10 NLT

When we are at a loss for what to do, do we turn to the Lord? It's good to get advice from others, and it's not a bad idea to weigh our decisions with the wisdom of trusted advisors. Jesus is the ultimate advisor. He always knows what we need, and he always has a solution.

The wisdom of Christ comes through personal fellowship with his Spirit, through others who speak his truth, and through the Word of God. The fruit of his wisdom is this: pure, peace-loving, gentle, willing to yield to others, full of mercy and good deeds, sincere, and without favoritism (James 3:17). These are attributes and not hard-and-fast rules. Knowing the nature of Christ will help us follow the fruit of his character in our decisions.

Jesus, I look to you whenever I have a need. When I don't know what to do, speak to me. When I can't hear your voice clearly, may I follow the steps in front of me. You will direct me as I go.

GOOD GOD

"If your children ask for bread,
which of you would give them a stone?"
MATTHEW 7:9 NCV

Any decent parent, when their child says they are hungry, would feed them to the best of their ability. When we ask God to meet our needs, do we wait for him to offer us a punishment instead? God is a good father. He is the best father. Even if our earthly parents failed us in every way imaginable, they are not a reflection of the goodness of God. He is trustworthy, kind, and patient. He always follows through. He is reliable and loving.

Who are the trustworthy people in your life? The ones who show up when you need them, take your calls in the middle of the night, know your good, bad, and boring sides, and love you through it all? They are gifts of God and representations of his love for you, yet he is infinitely better. Use these people to launch your understanding of God's limitless love.

Jesus, I want to know you more in truth, experience, and expectation. Thank you for providing for my needs. I know I can trust you and rest in that trust.

PERSPECTIVES OF PEACE

"When you hear of wars and rumors of wars,
don't be alarmed; these things must take place,
but it is not yet the end."
MARK 13:7 CSB

Even when there is not peace in the world, we can have peace in our hearts. When we hear about bad things happening, let's not panic. Jesus warned us these things would happen. There is suffering in this world, and we can't escape it. However, we can reach out in mercy, generosity, and peace. We can be promoters of God's kingdom values even when the world wars against them.

How do we do this? We live the way Jesus taught us to. We humbly follow the example of Christ, rely on the graceful strength of the Spirit, and remain clothed in compassion. The peace of God transcends human understanding; it can calm the greatest storm within us even when the storms around us still rage.

Jesus, you are the Prince of Peace. You are where my heart finds rest. When I am alarmed by the state of the world, I will remember your words of warning and the promise of your presence through it all. Help me push forward in your strength and grace.

STEP OUT

"It is not the healthy who need a doctor,
but the sick."
Luke 5:31 NIV

Jesus came to save the sinner, bring the lost home, and heal the sick. How often do we let his love lead us to the edges of society, or even just out of our little comfort zones, to extend practical kindness to those who need it?

It is not our place to judge those who struggle. We have access to Christ's compassion, and compassion does not drive us into isolation; it invites us to connect. The roots of tradition in religion can keep us from reaching out the way Christ calls us to. If we walk in the steps of Christ, we will find ourselves in situations where others question our choice of companions or the work we choose to do. The Son of God did not think himself too holy to have meals with those others hated. Are we courageous enough to do the same?

Jesus, I don't ever want to question whether kindness is worth my reputation. Help me follow your ways knowing I will be misunderstood by some, and that's okay. Your gospel is worth it, and so is the power of your love reaching every person.

CONSIDER THE TIMING

"My time has not yet come,
but your time is always ready."
JOHN 7:6 NKJV

Have you ever been told what you should be doing to get ahead in life? Perhaps you have heard that going to a certain place, following a certain strategy, or dressing a certain way will lead you to success. Even Jesus' brothers gave unsolicited advice.

Jesus didn't let their pestering get to him. He knew it was not the right time for him to go to Judea even if it didn't make sense to his brothers. When you have conviction about your path, knowing the timing is as important as the steps you take. Don't be discouraged by the impatience of others. Don't let their skepticism rush you. Know the season you are in and find your confidence in the deep wisdom guiding you. Turn their pressure back on them and let them know they can follow that path if they like, but you know what is right for you now.

Jesus, thank you for this example of you standing your ground against those trying to pressure you into something you knew wasn't right. I take my courage from your conviction, and I stand my ground without shame.

FRUIT OF ACTION

"You will know them by their fruits."
MATTHEW 7:20 NASB

How we live displays what we believe. As Jesus said in verses 17-18 of this same chapter, "every good tree bears good fruit, but the bad tree bears bad fruit. A good tree cannot bear bad fruit" and vice versa. We will be known by the legacy of our choices, actions, and relationships.

Just as we recognize an apple tree by the fruit it bears, so can we recognize someone who lives in the love of Christ. We are the branches connected to the vine, Jesus. Those who are not in the vine do not bear his fruit. The actions of those in Christ will display the nature of God as the fruit of his Spirit. It's that simple.

Lord, I abide in your love. I want every part of my life to reflect your mercy, redemption, and grace. I choose to grow in the light of your truth. May the fruit of my life honor you.

HE KNOWS

Jesus said to him, "Truly, I tell you, this very night,
before the rooster crows twice,
you will deny me three times."
MARK 14:30 ESV

Peter was sure he could stand strong in his love for the
Lord in the face of persecution. Jesus had just told his
disciples they would fall away and scatter. Peter resisted
and said, "Even if they do, I will not." Jesus, both gracious
and honest, told Peter the truth: he would deny Jesus
three times before the morning came.

Peter did not want to think himself so weak as to deny
the teacher and friend he loved. However, we know Peter
did deny Jesus three times. This was a humbling moment
for Peter, yet how gracious that Jesus told him the truth.
Pride goes before a fall. Peter lived this, and so do we. Even
in our falling, God already knew we would do it, and he
offers us grace, mercy, and restoration.

Jesus, thank you for knowing my limits and faults and
loving me through them even when I am unwilling to
confront them. I remain humble in your mercy. Lead me
in your truth and restore me in your kindness.

HARVEST IS HERE

"The harvest is huge and ripe. But there are not enough harvesters to bring it all in. As you go, plead with the Owner of the Harvest to drive out into his harvest fields many more workers."
LUKE 10:2 TPT

When we are overworked and we realize that we have more opportunities than resources to reach them, what other choice do we have but to seek help? In the kingdom of God, there is a harvest ready, but there aren't enough harvesters to bring it in. We can ask the Lord to call many more to go into the ripe fields and bring in the return on his good news.

What part do we play in this? Are we being obedient to the call of God to love others unconditionally, speak the truth, and stand for justice? Are we serving as the hands and feet of Jesus in a world of people longing for a loving touch? As we seek to answer these questions, may we partner with the God of the harvest.

Jesus, I am reminded of a vision in Isaiah. He heard the Lord say, "Whom shall we send, and who will go for us?" His response was, "Here am I, Lord. Send me!" Well, Lord. Here I am. Send me.

BE ON YOUR GUARD

"Remember that I am sending you out
as lambs among wolves."
LUKE 10:3 NLT

Even though we may feel vulnerable going into spaces
and places that are unfamiliar to us God goes with us. He
is the one we trust. However, we must remember we are
lambs, and there are wolves around. These predators are
not always easy to spot from a cursory glance. This is why
Jesus advised his followers to be "as shrewd as snakes
and harmless as doves" (Matthew 10:16). Jesus went on
to warn that they would be handed over to courts and
flogged in synagogues; the abusers were those who
claimed to know and love God.

Wisdom tells us to be on our guard. Wisdom leads to
discernment. Knowing the nature of God, we can discern
who is actually living for him and who has got the wrong
idea about who he is.

Jesus, it is easy to forget that not all people who claim
to know you actually do. Make me wise to their schemes.
I will follow you even when others react poorly.

LINGERING LOVE

> "I loved you as the Father loved me.
> Now remain in my love."
> JOHN 15:9 NCV

Jesus loves us the way the Father loves him. What is told as past tense in this account can be traded for present because we know God is love. Unbound by the constraints of our humanity, his love reaches through space and time. We see the lived-out love of Christ toward his followers. This is the love we choose to remain in. This is the lingering love of the triune God—Father, Son, and Spirit—to us.

As Christ has loved us, so let us love one another. In practical ways, we can remain in his love by choosing to live it out today. Jesus goes on to say, "If you obey my commands, you will remain in my love" (15:10). In love and by the grace and power of his Spirit, we can live as he instructed.

Christ, thank you for the power of your Spirit which enables me to remain in your love as I align my actions with your teachings. You are my source of strength and joy.

INDIFFERENCE

"To what should I compare this generation?
It's like children sitting in the marketplaces
who call out to other children:
We played the flute for you,
but you didn't dance;
we sang a lament,
but you didn't mourn!"
MATTHEW 11:16-17 CSB

When we turn a blind eye and deaf ear to people trying to share their experiences with us, we distance ourselves from the compassion of Christ. Indifference is not a value of the kingdom. Have you tried to share a vulnerable aspect of yourself with someone only to have a wall go up between you? It was not your bid at connection, but their refusal to connect, that was a problem.

We can't meet the needs of everyone around us, but we can make room for their experiences. We can validate. We can mourn with those who mourn and celebrate with those who are rejoicing. There is space for all of it.

Jesus, I want to remain open to connection with others even when it means hearing uncomfortable experiences that don't align with my own. Your love breaks down barriers; it doesn't put them up.

SECRET TREASURE

"The secret of the kingdom of God has been given to you. But to those on the outside everything is said in parables."

MARK 4:11 NIV,

Those who are spiritually hungry look for the hidden meaning of the parables of Christ. They seek to know the underlying truths about God's kingdom through the stories that Jesus told. The hungry will be fed, and the thirsty will be satisfied.

If we have a driving hunger in our hearts to truly grasp the wisdom of Christ, we will find the secret treasures of God's ways. Isaiah 45:3 says, "I will give you hidden treasures, riches stored in secret places, so that you may know that I am the Lord." These hidden treasures are found in Christ.

Lord, my heart longs to know you more. I won't give up learning your ways, for I know I have not grasped them all. Continue to teach and correct me. Lead me to riches stored in the secret places of your presence.

IMMENSE JOY

"There is joy in the presence of the angels of God
over one sinner who repents."
LUKE 15:10 NKJV

There is a wonderful, joyous celebration in heaven every time a lost son or daughter repents and turns to God. God is full of emotion. He does not simply add a number to a running tally; he celebrates every single restored soul.

Have you tempered your own joy and celebration thinking that God is serious? Think again. He delights in your triumphs. Don't hold back from celebrating a victory no matter how insignificant it may seem to someone else. Call a close friend, go out to dinner, make a cake, or have a dance party. Whatever celebrating looks like to you, let your immense joy take over.

Joyful Jesus, I'm glad you weren't (and still aren't) overly serious. You know how to get down to business, and you also know how to enjoy life. I am still learning how to give joy a rightful place in my life. As I celebrate the little victories, teach me to rejoice like you do.

LIFE GIVING NOURISHMENT

"The bread of God is that which comes down out of
heaven and gives life to the world."
JOHN 6:33 NASB

When the Israelites were wandering in the desert after
their deliverance from Egypt, God provided bread from
heaven each morning to satisfy the hunger of the people.
This manna from heaven was not Moses' provision; it was
the Father's gift.

In an even bigger show of provision, the Father gave Jesus,
providing the ultimate way to experience the abundance
of his kingdom. Jesus also said we do not live on bread
alone but on every word that comes from God. Jesus is the
very Word of God made flesh. He is our sustenance, life-
giving nourishment, and strength. Let's receive the manna
of his presence every morning. He is all we need and more
than enough to satisfy our souls.

Bread of Life, you are the one I come to every day
for fresh revelation, understanding, and strength.
I need you more than I can express. Thank you for
the sufficiency of your life-giving presence.

TRANSPARENT AND TRUE

"Father, your plan delights your heart, as you've chosen this way to extend your kingdom—by giving it to those who have become like trusting children."
MATTHEW 11:26 TPT

God does not reveal his authority to those who are wise in their own eyes. People who think they already know it all are not open to receiving more. To those who humble themselves, God reveals the extent of his kingdom power.

How willingly do we trust our heavenly Father? No matter how confident we are today, we can still come to him like children. We can humble our hearts before him. We can be completely honest with him. Think of the lack of filter most children have. Jesus said we should come to him like children, so let's come with our guards down and our curiosity leading. He will meet us with the wisdom of his kingdom and satisfy our hunger with his provision.

Loving Jesus, thank you for the delight you find in children. I recognize how little I know as the façade of control I have over my life gives way. I trust you even though there is so much I don't understand.

EMBRACE THE INNOCENT

"Whoever receives one such child in my name
receives me, and whoever receives me,
receives not me but him who sent me."
MARK 9:37 ESV

When we receive a child in the name of Christ, there is an expectation of honor. Jesus said that whoever welcomes a child in his name actually welcomes him, and those who welcome him welcome the Father. How we treat children directly reflects how we treat God.

With this in mind, how can we welcome children with an openness that honors where they are and the growth they haven't yet achieved? Children are not to be overlooked, left on their own, or abused. They are to be nurtured and protected. We can love the little ones in our lives and in this world with the connection Jesus made; we are loving God himself.

Jesus, increase my understanding of your kingdom as I submit to loving those dependent on adults. Thank you for the perspective you gave. Help me rise to the challenge as I step outside of myself and into purposeful connection with others.

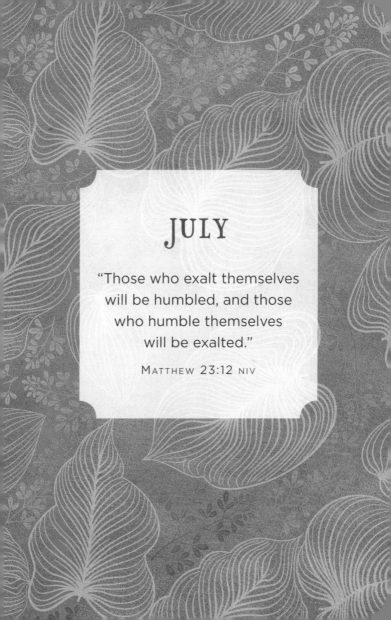

JULY

"Those who exalt themselves
will be humbled, and those
who humble themselves
will be exalted."

MATTHEW 23:12 NIV

ROOTED IN COMPASSION

"You hypocrites! Each of you works on the Sabbath day!
Don't you untie your ox or your donkey from its stall on
the Sabbath and lead it out for water? This dear woman,
a daughter of Abraham, has been held in bondage by
Satan for eighteen years. Isn't it right that she be released,
even on the Sabbath?"

LUKE 13:15-16 NLT

Hypocrisy has no place in the kingdom of Christ. If we use
one standard to measure ourselves while holding others
to a different standard, we are hypocrites. Classism, sexism,
racism, and elitism do not belong to God, and he never
condones any of it. With his help, we can move in radical
humility and mercy rather than make excuses for why our
religious traditions mean more than the words of Christ.

There is so much mercy to meet us when we admit our
wrongs and are willing to correct them. When we repent,
the kindness of Christ washes over us. May we always
humble ourselves before him rather than defend our
loveless actions.

Jesus, may my life be rooted in compassion. May I never
defend those who use your Word to justify their hatred
of others. Thank you for meeting me with your grace
and mercy every time I humble myself before you.

HIGHER WISDOM

"The things I teach are not my own,
but they come from him who sent me."
JOHN 7:16 NCV

The teachings of Jesus are not just the thoughts of a nice Middle Eastern man who lived two thousand years ago. The truth he spoke was the truth of the God of the Ages. He revealed the nature of the Father in more meaningful ways than any before him. His radical stance on mercy, justice, and humility was, and remains, in direct contrast to how many perceived God before this.

We are limited in our knowledge of the Father, but we have the Spirit to testify to his overwhelmingly faithful nature. His loyal love washes over us and fills us with the transformative power of his presence. We can trust Jesus' perspective. He is still revealing the Father to us through his Spirit today.

Jesus, thank you for the power of your presence in my life. You reveal the heart of the Father through your life, words, and miraculous ministry. I rely on your perspective to teach and lead me in this life.

DRINK DEEPLY

"The one who believes in me, as the Scripture has said, will
have streams of living water flow from deep within him."
JOHN 7:38 CSB

Deep within our innermost beings, the Spirit of God flows
within us. The living waters of God's presence flood our
hearts and minds. If you are thirsty for more of the Lord
today, you have only to come and drink.

The presence of God is not dripped out in careful pours. It
overflows from the heart of the Father like a waterfall after
spring rains. It washes over you in overwhelming measure,
and out of your heart will flow the rivers of his life. Drink
deeply of his love, rest in the shade of his presence, and
find your inner being refreshed in his delight today. He is
the source of living water, and he will satisfy your soul.

Jesus, you are the ultimate source of my peace, joy, love,
patience, strength, and overwhelming hope. I come to
drink deeply of your presence. Satisfy my soul with your
perfect love.

LIBERATED BY GOD

"If the Son sets you free,
you will be free indeed."
JOHN 8:36 NIV

If you have found your liberation in Christ, you are truly free. The sin that kept you trapped in cycles of fear, shame, and lack, is no longer your master; Christ is. With Christ's perfection as your own, you are free to live in the abundance of his mercy. You are free, as all children are, to make mistakes, learn, and grow from them.

What Christ does not hold against us, we must learn to lay down too. Psalm 103:12 says, "As far as the east is from the west, so far has he removed our transgressions from us." As far as the sunrise is from the sunset, he has removed our sins. We need never take them up again.

Liberator, you have purified me, set me free, and given me a new lease on life. Thank you for the liberty of your love that allows me to start over in your mercy as often as I receive it. Create lasting change in me as I come alive in your presence.

EVERYONE EVERYWHERE

"The gospel must first be preached to all the nations."
MARK 13:10 NKJV

Every nation, people, and language will have the opportunity to hear about the love of Christ through the spread of the gospel. This is what Jesus says must happen before the end of this age. He won't return until it's done.

What does it mean to preach the gospel to all nations? Does preaching only happen with words, or is it through the lived-out love of Christ's ways that others can see him as the way, the truth, and the life? Jesus said we would do even greater things than he did. This means that miracles are part of the spread of the gospel. Instead of boiling it down to a formula, let's get creative about the expressions of Christ's good news that we can share through our unique gifts, talents, and expressions.

Jesus, you are the King of all, and you will receive the honor and glory you are due. I want to spread your love to others. Show me how to follow you in authenticity and express the truth of your good news through my life.

BEYOND THE SUPERFICIAL

"Stop judging based on the superficial. First you must
embrace the standards of mercy and truth."
JOHN 7:24 TPT

The law of God's love is more important than the law of
Moses. The law of mercy supersedes what was formerly
given to Moses because it is the expression and command
that Jesus Christ gave on the Father's behalf. Though the
law of Moses said no one could be healed on the Sabbath,
Jesus was clear that the mercy of God always wins out
over traditions that keep us from loving action.

If we are to stop judging others based on the superficial,
we must also stop judging our actions based on the
regulations of an outdated system. Jesus fulfilled the law
of Moses and rendered some of its uses obsolete. He gave
us a new command: to love God with all our souls, hearts,
minds, and strength, and to love our neighbors as we love
ourselves. If we do that, we won't go wrong.

Lord, I can see how offensive you must have been to
the religious leaders of your day. I confess I feel offense
at some of your teachings too. But I want to know you,
walk in the light of your mercy, and truly understand
your kingdom.

REMEMBER YOUR PURPOSE

"I must also preach the kingdom of God to the other cities, because I was sent for this purpose."

LUKE 4:43 NASB

Jesus did not lose sight of the purpose of his ministry even amidst of a crowd of people begging him to stay with them. He found favor in Capernaum, but he was not lulled or deterred by this fact. We must also be unflappable in our purpose when tempted to stay in a place of comfort and ease.

Jesus also spent time praying in seclusion. By prioritizing time alone with God, we don't lose focus of who we are or what we've been called to do. Grounded in fellowship with God through personal prayer, worship, and reading his Word, we can keep our purpose in sight.

Jesus, you were there at the beginning, you were there when I was created, and you know my purpose as well as the Father. As I make spending time with you a priority, refine my vision and the focus of my efforts. Thank you for your help.

REVELATIONS OF TRUTH

"All things have been handed over to me by my Father,
and no one knows the Son except the Father,
and no one knows the Father except the Son
and anyone to whom the Son chooses to reveal him."
MATTHEW 11:27 ESV

The only way we come to know the Father is through Jesus Christ. He reveals the heart of the Father to us, and we enter into fullness of relationship with him through the death, resurrection, and redemption of Christ. His mercy is our covering so we can boldly come to the throne of grace.

Before we go searching for truth in society, let's go to Jesus. His work is vast, and God's fingerprints are everywhere: science, nature, all kinds of communities, and in you. Look to Jesus when you have questions and listen for his voice in the world as much as you do in sanctuaries or churches. He is faithful to reveal himself wherever you are.

Lord, your truth is more generous and vast than any one mind, group of people, or theological concept can hold. Help me see your truth in the world, for you are not confined by the spaces I make for you.

REWARDS OF HOSPITALITY

"If anyone gives you even a cup of water because you
belong to the Messiah, I tell you the truth,
that person will surely be rewarded."
MARK 9:41 NLT

Any act of hospitality done in the name of Christ will
receive a reward. We store for ourselves treasures in
heaven as we welcome the outsider, care for the orphan
and widow, feed the hungry, and house the poor. May we
be radical in our generosity knowing that it reflects the
marvelous mercy of God.

How can you bless others in practical ways today? Pay
for someone else's coffee. Help someone who looks like
they need a hand. Be more generous than you normally
would and try to outdo yourself tomorrow. Do it with
compassion knowing you will receive your reward from
your Father. He sees every movement in mercy. Help your
brothers and sisters in the faith, but don't stop there. Be
kind to everyone.

**Jesus Christ, as your follower, I will look for ways to
encourage my brothers and sisters in Christ. Give me
eyes to see needs I can fill. Teach me to love others the
way you love each of us: unconditionally.**

STAY TRUE

"I have this against you:
You have left the love you had in the beginning."
REVELATION 2:4 NCV

When we stand face-to-face with God in the end, we will give an account of our lifestyles and choices. Feeling confident in your current situation? Even those who continue to walk in the ways of God can fall into the trap of losing the love that first drew them to Christ. We can persevere through many trials and still lose our passionate love for God.

This is what Christ was referring to in this letter we call Revelation. We must keep the fire of love burning in our hearts. How? By staying connected to the source of love. We cultivate hearts of love to fuel our choices and keep us coming back to the one who rescued us from the shackles of shame. The love of God flows toward us even now. Let it wash away weariness, doubt, bitterness, and confusion.

Jesus, my heart is yours. Revive me in the living waters of your presence and refresh my perspective in the wisdom of your mercy. I love you, and I am growing in love for you.

SEIZE EVERY OPPORTUNITY

"I'm glad for you that I wasn't there so that you may believe. But let's go to him."

JOHN 11:15 CSB

The implication in this verse is that if Jesus had been with Lazarus, he wouldn't have died. He felt the grief of the family as well as his own. However, we know Jesus purposefully didn't visit earlier. He saw the opportunity to increase the faith of those who would witness the resurrection of Lazarus.

In every dark time and loss, there is an opportunity to watch the power of Jesus meet us. He is kind, comforting, and strong. Do we trust that what Jesus says, he will do? He follows through in faithfulness every time. Even when our hearts break, he reveals the mercy of the Father to us. Many losses don't end with miraculous resurrection, but the miracle of Jesus' fellowship is ours nonetheless. May we await his presence and look for the light of his love that shines no matter how dark the grief.

Jesus, you can raise the dead, and I know you can heal my broken heart too. Whatever you will, I submit to you. Show me where your mercy enters into my pain. I trust you.

SPIRIT'S POWER

"You will receive power when the Holy Spirit comes on you; and you will be my witnesses in Jerusalem, and in all Judea and Samaria, and to the ends of the earth."

ACTS 1:8 NIV

The Holy Spirit's presence was not just for New Testament Christians to experience. The promise of the Spirit was to all who believe in Christ, and that includes each of us. We don't need to strive to know God, and we don't need to be strong enough on our own.

The Spirit comes to us, makes his home within us, and revives us from the inside out. The power of the Spirit is the same power that raised Christ from the dead and moved in mighty miracles through Jesus' ministry healing the sick, freeing the tormented, and humbling the arrogant. This power fuels our passion for God and his kingdom purposes. We wait on the Spirit knowing that when he moves, we will be moved to follow.

Jesus, thank you for the gift of your Spirit. He allows me to experience the depths of your love, the power of your presence, and the wisdom of your teaching. I am grateful for his sweet companionship.

PRIORITIES

"As you go, preach, saying,
'The kingdom of heaven is at hand.'"
MATTHEW 10:7 NKJV

The kingdom of heaven is coming sooner than we anticipate. We know how fleeting life is. When death touches us, we understand this more clearly. We are here one minute and gone the next. How we live matters, and no one is guaranteed a limitless future on this earth.

How should we live? We live to honor God through our loving submission to his ways. We prioritize relationships, legacies, and important things in this life. When we live with the reality of Christ's kingdom in sight, we can align our choices in Jesus' ways with less hesitation. Let go of things that don't matter and focus on the significant.

Lord Jesus, help me keep the vision of your kingdom at hand. I don't want to waste my days living for fleeting things that don't matter. Refresh my focus in your love and give me understanding so I can prioritize well.

ALMIGHTY GOD

"The most important of all the commandments is this:
'The Lord Yahweh, our God, is one!'"

MARK 12:29 TPT

Yahweh, the God of the prophets, of Abraham, Moses, and David, is the one and only Lord over all. He is the Creator, and no one compares to him. He is worthy of our devotion, adoration, and trust. He is full of loyal love, constant peace, and perfect justice. He will not fail, and he will not falter.

When we have a right perspective of God, we can honor him not only with what we say but with how we live. After a glimpse of the glory of God, who can remain the same? Moses was forever changed by his encounter with the burning bush, and David experienced the merciful help of God over and over again. To love God well, we must know him, and we can get to know him through Christ and the Spirit. He has already offered us all we need. What a gracious and generous God he is!

Yahweh, thank you for the lengths you went to, and still go to, in love to reveal the truth of your nature. I worship you.

YOU WILL SEE

"What I am doing, you do not realize right now,
but you will understand later."
JOHN 13:7 NASB

We cannot always understand what God is up to in the moment. We may fear he doesn't see us in our pain or confusion, but he is with us. There is more at work within the world than God's purposes. There are many factors that affect us, but he is aware of them all.

Rest in the words of Jesus. Even if we don't currently realize what Jesus is doing, or the significance of it, we will understand later. How many of us, through hindsight, have spotted the wisdom of God through our lives? He weaves the thread of his mercy through the details. Let's trust him even if we are confused or upset at the moment. He is faithful, and everything he does is with purpose.

Jesus, when I can't understand your ways and your work is difficult to glimpse in my life, I wrestle to trust. Meet me now with your overwhelming peace and speak to my soul. I need you.

NO USE HIDING

"Is a lamp brought in to be put under a basket,
or under a bed, and not on a stand?"
MARK 4:21 ESV

A lamp is not turned on and then hidden. We turn on a light to use it. Jesus says everything that is hidden will eventually be brought out into the open. No secret will remain obscured from sight. He is the light that shines in the darkness, and we can't hide what God sees.

There is no fear, shame, or sin that can separate us from the love of God in Christ. He lights up our lives and reveals what needs to be confessed and corrected. When we turn from our sins and repent, he is faithful to forgive us every time. Live in the pure light of his presence and share in the fellowship of his mercy which cleanses all sin.

Glorious Lord, there is no shadow in you. You don't have hidden ulterior motives, and you aren't motivated by greed, power, or fear. You are love, and in your love, I come alive. I want to shine for you.

WISE BUILDERS

"Anyone who listens to my teaching and follows it is wise,
like a person who builds a house on solid rock."
MATTHEW 7:24 NLT

When we build our lives on the rock of Jesus' teachings,
we have a firm foundation. With a solid foundation, we
can focus on building. We have confidence and stability
because God's faithfulness undergirds everything we do.

A wise builder does not just think about the aesthetics
of the final building; they plan from the bottom up and
ensue the foundation laid is solid and the structure of the
home is well-built. We are foolish if we think we can dress
up exteriors without dealing with the inner work that
must be attended to. The power of Christ deals with the
whole of a person, so let's be sure to lay foundations and
tend to the structure of our inner lives with care, honesty,
and wisdom.

Jesus, you are the rock on which I build my life. Your
ways are the ways I choose to follow. Transform my life
in your wisdom, and as I submit to you, may the roots of
my heart, intentions, and purposes grow deep in the soil
of your love.

SOLID FOUNDATION

"It rained hard, the floods came, and the winds blew and hit that house. But it did not fall, because it was built on rock. Everyone who hears my words and does not obey them is like a foolish man who built his house on sand."

MATTHEW 7:25-26 NCV

When we don't listen or put the words of Christ into practice, we are like shortsighted people who build a house on sand. When the winds and waves come, the house will topple. What we build our lives on matters.

The solid foundation of Christ's kingdom ways is a tried-and-true way to succeed in life. When the storms of life blow, the house will not tumble. When we choose to live with generosity, mercy, justice, and humility, we nurture a set of values rooted in the strength of Christ. His ways do not expire, nor does the power of his kingdom. May our foundation be set on the solid rock of Christ. Then, we have no need to worry about the future.

Jesus, I don't want to be shortsighted or foolish in my choices. Thank you for your grace that empowers me to choose your ways. I trust you know better than I do. Your love is never wrong.

OPEN–HANDED GENEROSITY

"Give to everyone who asks you, and from someone who
takes your things, don't ask for them back."
Luke 6:30 csb

The ways of Jesus are wildly different from the ways of
this world. "Give to everyone who begs from you" is not
even something you will often hear preached from a
pulpit! When we recognize our resources as gifts from
our generous Father, we can more easily offer to others
without fear of what will happen to us. Our Father is a
good provider, and he sees all we give.

We must not hold on to our resources so tightly that the
act of giving becomes a sacrifice. Let's practice generosity
and strengthen it like a muscle. Giving to those who beg is
one way to do this. If someone takes what is ours, our first
reaction is to demand it back, but Jesus instructs us to let
it go. Our Father, who sees what is done, will restore what
we have lost. It's a counter-cultural act of trust.

Jesus, I want to be more generous than I am. Help me
practice generosity and build the muscle of giving
without expecting anything in return. This is how
you are, and I want to reflect you.

HOLDING ON

"You have let go of the commands of God
and are holding on to human traditions."
MARK 7:8 NIV

What is more important to you: your traditions, way of doing things, and current understanding, or what God says? If we hold too tightly to our biases and preferences, we may miss out on what God is doing. Many of the religious leaders of Jesus' day certainly did.

It is a practice of surrender and humility to admit when we are wrong and ask for forgiveness. It is a practice of courage and trust to then change how we approach these things. Traditions can be powerful, but they can also be restrictive if we favor them instead of following the Lord to lead. We need to hold more tightly to Christ than we do the way we first came to Christ.

Jesus, I don't want to hold more tightly to what is expected rather than to what you say. I choose to follow you no matter what. Keep my heart humble and pliable in your love.

THE WAY

"I am the way, the truth, and the life.
No one comes to the Father except through Me."
JOHN 14:6 NKJV

Through Jesus, we find the way to the Father who welcomes us with open arms. Like the father of the prodigal son, he embraces us as we turn to him. He wraps his royal robes around us and celebrates our homecoming. In his arms, we find true acceptance, love, and joy. There is freedom, peace, and a future in his abundant kingdom.

Jesus is the truth. Anything that counters his teachings, ministry, and resurrection power must give way under his authority. We must look to him more than we look to the traditions of religion. May we come to him more often than we go to any other. There is an open door to the presence of the Father through him, and there we find our invigorating life.

Jesus, you are the way, the truth, and the life. I come to the Father through you with the help of the Holy Spirit. Thank you for all you are, all you do, and all you stand for. I am yours.

EYES THAT SEE

"To you it has been granted to know the mysteries of the kingdom of God, but to the rest they are told in parables, so that while seeing they may not see, and while hearing they may not understand."

LUKE 8:10 NASB

What does it take to be in this category of people Jesus was speaking to? It takes an openness to listen, a hunger for the truth, and a willingness to put knowledge into action. With teachable hearts, we can "perceive the secret, hidden mysteries of God's kingdom realm," as it says in the Passion Translation's version of this verse.

Do you have eyes that see who Jesus is? Do you have ears that understand what he is saying? Jesus is alive, and he is still moving in the world and in our lives. The Spirit reveals his truths to our hearts, and we find living fellowship in his presence. May we not give up spending time with him in prayer, reading his Word, and living out his teachings.

Lord Jesus, give me eyes to see and ears to ear. May my heart remain teachable as you reveal the ways of your kingdom and I put them into practice. You are full of liberating truth and astounding love.

HEAVENLY TREASURES

"Do not lay up for yourselves treasures on earth,
where moth and rust destroy
and where thieves break in and steal."
MATTHEW 6:19 ESV

We cannot take our wealth with us when we leave this earth. When our bodies fail and our breath stops, nothing carries over with us into eternity. The pharaohs of Egypt were buried with their belongings thinking they would need them for the afterlife. However, when their tombs are uncovered, we find that those things remain.

There is a kind of treasure we can store up for ourselves that moth and rust don't destroy, and thieves can't steal. Heavenly treasures, the eternal realities that never change, can be found in how we treat others, how generously we live and give, doing good, and sharing the truth of God's love. No one can take these things from us, and the values of our lives reverberate into eternity.

King Jesus, I align myself in your kingdom love, and I choose to put my efforts into the values you taught us. I want my life to matter for more than the few decades I get on this earth. Thank you for a future and a hope in your kingdom.

FOR ALL PEOPLE

"Does not the Scripture say, 'My house will be
a house of prayer for all the world to share'?
But you have made it a thieves' hangout!"
MARK 11:17 TPT

According to Isaiah 56:7, God says, "my house of worship
will be known as a house of prayer for all people." All
are welcome in the kingdom of God, and all should be
welcome in the temple of his presence on the earth. It is
not for us to exclude anyone from God's family.

Today's verse is in same passage where Jesus flipped the
tables in the temple. He rebuked the people for using a
place dedicated to worship God for commerce. Greed has
no place in God's house, but unfortunately it shows up
more often than we like to admit. We must look for ways
to widen our reach and our generosity by breaking down
walls of exclusion and by refusing to profit on the gospel
of Christ.

Jesus, your love is given freely to all who will receive it. This
doesn't mean it's cheap; your love cost you everything.
Thank you for your incredible generosity. May I walk in
your generous ways and refuse to promote exclusivity
and commerce over relationships within your church.

IN THE OPEN

"All that is secret will eventually be brought into the open,
and everything that is concealed will be brought to light
and made known to all."

Luke 8:17 NLT

It is wise to live as if we have nothing to hide. With integrity as a guiding value, we can remain authentic, honest, and humble. Is there something you've been afraid to share with those close to you? Consider sharing it or, to put it another way, bringing it into the light. Be sure to do this with someone you trust.

If that feels like too big of a jump today, offer it to the Lord. Be open about your struggles, your questions, and your longings. Nothing is too much for him to handle. He welcomes you as you are, and if correction is needed, he always does it in kindness. After all, it is his kindness that leads us to repentance.

Jesus, thank you for the kindness of your correction and for the strength of your love for me. I don't want to keep anything from you, and I want to live more fully and freely in my relationships. Give me the courage to do this.

SPIRITUAL BIRTH

"I tell you the truth, unless you are born from water
and the Spirit, you cannot enter God's kingdom."
JOHN 3:5 NCV

To experience the abundant spiritual life God created us
for, we must be "born from Spirit." This is a rebirth, and
it's where we get the term "born again." The Spirit of God
breathes into us as he did in the beginning with Adam. His
breath fills us with life.

The kingdom of God is experienced by those spiritually
renewed in the incredible mercy of Christ. The Spirit, like
wind, cannot be seen, captured, or manipulated. The Spirit
breathes, and we are moved. We feel the refreshing winds
of his presence. This Spirit ushers us into the kingdom of
heaven where God dwells. Here, we come alive from the
inside out, for the Spirit makes his home in us.

Lord, thank you for the hope of your kingdom. Please
send your Spirit to renew and baptize me in your
incredible mercy.

SUPERNATURAL LIFE

"The natural realm can only give birth
to things that are natural, but the spiritual
realm gives birth to supernatural life!"
JOHN 3:6 TPT

Are you looking to change your ways, experience more satisfaction in life, or feel a greater purpose? We can only do so much on our own, but the Spirit of God offers us the power of his transformative love to work wonders for our souls.

We can't avoid suffering in this life, but we can experience the peace of God no matter what is going on. Jesus said, "The spiritual realm gives birth to supernatural life." Through fellowship with him, we know the overwhelming, supernatural goodness of his life within us. Paul said in Colossians 1:27, "Living within you is the Christ who floods you with the expectation of glory! The mystery of Christ, embedded within us, becomes a heavenly treasure chest of hope filled with the riches of glory for his people." This treasure chest of hope belongs you.

Jesus, fill me up with your powerful love and transform my heart, soul, and mind. I long to walk in the ways of your Spirit.

WISE INNOCENCE

"I am sending you out like sheep among wolves.
Therefore be as shrewd as snakes and as innocent as doves."
MATTHEW 10:16 NIV

We face many obstacles in the world, but God does not ask us to stay in the safety of our comfortable lives. He teaches, prepares, and sends us out in his name. His presence always goes with us. He never leaves those who rely on him.

It is important we approach people with wisdom and discernment. While love always allows room for people to grow and prove us wrong, it is not fooled into thinking that everything in the world is right, fair, or just. We shouldn't expect smooth sailing, endless favor, or to be understood by everyone around us. It will be a quick lesson in disappointment if we do. We can be shrewd as snakes while also remaining as innocent as doves. We can hold the tension of discernment and mercy in our hands as we walk with Christ as our companion.

Lord Jesus, give me expectations grounded in truth. I don't want to be easily tricked. Train my heart in your discernment and help me stand on it while also leaving ample room for your mercy to move.

SIMPLY BELIEVE

"Have faith in God."
MARK 11:22 NKJV

Whenever Jesus performed a miracle, he didn't do it to impress others. He wanted people to believe in God and learn more about him. He wanted their faith to be strengthened by his marvelous miracles.

When we are astounded by the effects of Christ in our lives, let it signal us to have faith in God. Everything Jesus did, and does, has an effect in this natural world. His power is not a vague representation of the mystery of God's mercy; it is love made practical. It meets people in powerful, specific, and helpful ways. May we embrace the practicality of God's power that changes lives and moves mountains.

Jesus, I believe in you. Increase my faith as I trust you. Show yourself in marvelous works of mercy that meet me in the practicalities of life. I look to you.

WHO HE IS

While He was praying alone, the disciples were with Him,
and He questioned them, saying, "Who do the people
say that I am?"
LUKE 9:18 NASB

Before Jesus asked his disciples who they thought he was,
he made a point of asking what others said about him.
Whether this was intended for Jesus, the disciples, or both,
we know Jesus used it as a jumping-off point to deeper
conversation about what it means to follow him.

Though many believed Jesus was a powerful prophet,
Peter said Jesus was the Messiah. No matter what others
say about Jesus, what we think about him matters. If we
believe Jesus is the Messiah, we will follow the wisdom he
gave and align our lives with his values. If we truly believe
he is our Savior, then we can no longer live only to satisfy
ourselves.

Messiah, you are the way, the truth, and the life. It's
not just a belief system, either; I choose to change my
ways and correct my selfishness. Transform me from
the inside out.

TURN IT AROUND

Afterward Jesus found him in the temple and
said to him, "See, you are well! Sin no more,
that nothing worse may happen to you."
JOHN 5:14 ESV

God is generous in mercy. He does not manipulate us
in his love. He loves us because he loves us. He heals us
because he loves us. He transforms us because he loves us.
We have a part to play as well. We alone can choose our
response to his merciful kindness. Will we continue on as
before, or will we turn around and follow Jesus?

When we have a powerful encounter with the mercy of
Christ, we walk away transformed, but we are still human.
Rather than use our freedom to continue sinning, we can
turn away from the fear, shame, and wrongs we know
we shouldn't do. Jesus' statement wasn't a threat to the
healed man; it was a word of loving caution.

Jesus, I don't want to fall back into old ways of coping.
Keep me on the path of your grace and help me when
I slip. I won't hide from you, and I won't try to have my
own way. Your love is always better.

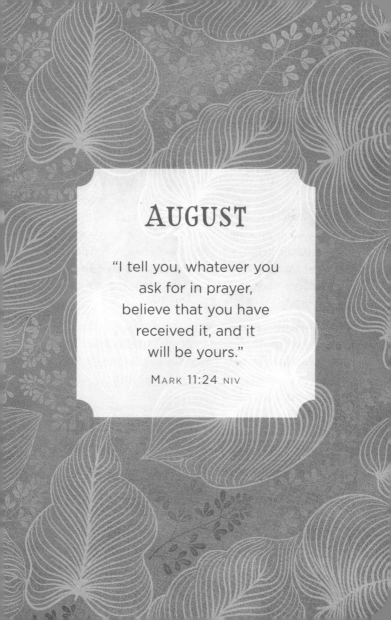

AUGUST

"I tell you, whatever you
ask for in prayer,
believe that you have
received it, and it
will be yours."

MARK 11:24 NIV

PERSISTENCE PAYS OFF

"Every persistent one will get what he asks for.
Every persistent seeker will discover what he longs for.
And everyone who knocks persistently will one day
find an open door."
MATTHEW 7:8 TPT

Do you recall the story of the persistent widow? In Luke 18, Jesus tells the parable about a woman who relentlessly pleaded case before a judge. Though he ignored her requests for a while, he was eventually worn down by her tenacity. She did not give up until the judge took her seriously.

How often do we give up at the smallest resistance? When we are passionate about something, we don't give up easily. No matter where you are in your journey today, if you have grown tired, rest—but don't give up! Your perseverance will pay off.

Jesus, thank you for pointing out how powerful persistence is. I don't want to give up on things that matter when others buck against it. Give me courage, endurance, and passion to continue.

LORD OVER ALL

"The Son of Man is Lord,
even over the Sabbath."
Luke 6:5 NLT

In today's passage, the Pharisees tried to put Jesus in his place by critiquing him and the disciples for picking grain on the Sabbath. Jesus responded by putting them in their place. Even King David, Jesus pointed out, ate from the bread in the sanctuary of God when he was hungry. This was against the law of the day, yet God did not hold it against him. Jesus went a step further and revealed he is the Son of Man, making him Lord over every other law.

How do we put Jesus in a box? Do we say what is his and what is not or refuse to recognize God's mercy is greater than our standards? We can't micromanage God. Let him expand your understanding of him as you encounter him in the world. He is greater than our limits, for he is the Son of Man and Lord over all.

Son of Man, thank you for being grander, wiser, and better than any of us could dream. Your mercy is not limited to my understanding of it; help me stop limiting what you are doing in love just because it doesn't match my rules and boxes.

MEANINGFUL SACRIFICE

"They gave only what they did not need.
This woman is very poor, but she gave all she had;
she gave all she had to live on."
MARK 12:44 NCV

Giving is an element of a good life. Even those who resist generosity will give when they know they can get a tax break in return. More than giving out of obligation, we must practice growing our generosity. We can build it like a muscle. The more intentional we are with it, the easier it will become to live that way.

In today's passage, the widow's offering was pure generosity and sacrifice. She gave out of what she needed to live while others gave out of the excess of their income. They did not feel the effects of their gift, but this widow did. It could have been the difference between her eating or not eating that day. When we are moved to give, let's do it as an act of loving sacrifice.

Lord, I don't want to hoard my belongings, money, or any other resource. Nurture in me the gift of giving generously. I choose to partner with your kingdom in willing sacrifice to you.

DON'T HIDE YOUR LIGHT

"You are the light of the world.
A city situated on a hill cannot be hidden."
"In the same way, let your light shine before others,
so that they may see your good works
and give glory to your Father in heaven."
MATTHEW 5:14, 16 CSB

What does it mean to be a light of the world? The Lord is the fire starter of our hearts, and our lives reflect his glorious mercy. We can't hide the love of God in us; it just doesn't work. His love shines brightly whether we are aware of it or not.

There is a reason Jesus says, "Shine your light before others, so that they may see your good works." When we align ourselves with his values, there is no mistaking to whom we belong. When we base our choices on Jesus' guidance, we choose his ways over the ways of this world. May the mercy of Christ to transform our thinking, choices, and priorities.

Radiant One, may my life reflect the wonders of your mercy so others may recognize the love of the Father. Your love has no limits, and I want to be radical in pursuing mercy, peace, and justice.

BLESSED

"Blessed are you who are poor,
for yours is the kingdom of God."
Luke 6:20 niv

Our bank accounts are not a reflection of God's favor. Neither are our families, jobs, or struggles. To be human is to face our limits. We can't think ourselves out of poverty. We can't hope ourselves out of trauma. Still, we know the mercy of God can transform our lives.

We may find immense gratitude in our circumstances, but let's not use our situations, good or bad, as excuses to withhold compassion, peace, or justice from those who need it. Blessed are those who struggle. Blessed are those who don't have an excess of resources. Theirs is the kingdom of God.

Jesus, forgive me for how I have judged others, and myself, on what they do or do not have. Your favor is more than a lucky circumstance; it is your very presence. I am blessed when I rely on you more than on earthly comforts.

FIRES OF TESTING

"Everyone will pass through the fire
and every sacrifice will be seasoned with salt."
MARK 9:49 TPT

None of us can avoid the testing that loss brings. We can't avoid pain, grief, or suffering. If we could, what a different experience life would be! We do have hope for this kind of life in the kingdom of Christ when it is fully established on earth as it is in heaven. However, this kingdom is still to come.

The fires of life can refine or destroy us. When we yield to the process and let the grace of God burn away what holds us back, we will emerge from the fire purer than when we entered. The essence of what matters becomes clearer in the moments of life or death. May we embrace those things that do and let go of things that don't.

Jesus, you are a restorer and redeemer. You are with me in the fires of this life just as you were with Daniel's friends in the fiery furnace. Even when I can't feel your presence, don't leave me. May my life be refined and seasoned with you.

GREAT IN THE KINGDOM

"Among those born of women there is not a greater
prophet than John the Baptist; but he who is least in the
kingdom of God is greater than he."

LUKE 7:28 NKJV

Even the "least" in the kingdom of God are greater than
the most revered prophets. How can this be? John the
Baptist was a devout man who followed God in all he did.
Even so, he did not have the same free fellowship with the
Spirit that we now have access to.

The power of the Spirit in our lives changes everything.
The Spirit's presence comforts, heals, and reveals the
wisdom of Christ to our hearts. The presence of God is
promised to those who believe in Christ, and the promise
is a persistent one. Jesus said in John 14:26, "the Holy
Spirit, he will teach you all things, and bring to your
remembrance all things that I said to you." The Triune God
makes his home in those who love Christ and keep his
word. This is greatness: to know God and walk with his
constant fellowship.

Jesus, thank you for the gift of your Spirit with me. Fill
me with your presence and awaken my heart to your
voice. I want to know you, obey you, and dwell in your
love every moment of every day.

TESTING OTHERS

"I know your deeds and your labor and perseverance, and that you cannot tolerate evil people, and you have put those who call themselves apostles to the test, and they are not, and you found them to be false."

REVELATION 2:2 NASB

There is a difference between judging others based on outer things and testing those who claim to be followers of Christ based on the fruit of their lives. While judging is not our place as children of God, testing the character of those who want to lead others in the name of Christ shouldn't be labeled as the same.

What are the criteria of testing? The ways of Christ. The fruit of the Spirit is evident in the lives of those filled with the life of Christ. We can't ignore the effect a person has on those around them. If they lead with fear, manipulation, and shame, then they are false teachers, for that is not the way of Christ. We can boil it down to what is important; are people loved well, provided for, and encouraged to extend mercy to others? This is a good representation of Christ's ministry in a life.

Jesus, may I have courage to hold to your standard those who claim to love you—especially when they lead others. But start with me first, Lord. I want to bear good fruit.

PATIENT ENDURANCE

"I know you are enduring patiently and bearing up for my name's sake, and you have not grown weary."
REVELATION 2:3 ESV

Ease and comfort are not promised to those who follow Christ. Even so, it's worth it to follow him. No one else can make that choice for us. We must count the cost to choose his ways over the world's. We must choose whom we will serve, and it won't be easy.

Endurance is a fruit of the Spirit. Many translations call it patience while others call it longsuffering. Whatever the term used, the meaning is the same. Those who can withstand waiting periods of life, testing, and grief do so with the help of the Spirit. There is comfort for those who mourn. There is peace that passes all understanding. When the going gets tough, remember the presence of God persists within and for us.

Lord, I lean on your loyal love when all else fails me. Your presence is life to me, and it gives me courage to keep going in patient endurance. You are my strength and peace.

THE BLESSING OF MERCY

"God blesses those who are merciful,
for they will be shown mercy."
MATTHEW 5:7 NLT

There are many expressions of mercy. One definition from the Oxford dictionary says mercy is "compassion or forgiveness shown toward someone whom it is within one's power to punish or harm." When we are in a position of power over someone and choose to show compassion, we demonstrate mercy.

Withholding punishment from those who deserve it is at the core of mercy. God reveals his mercy toward us through Christ. Instead of punishing us for the wrongs we commit, he allows us into his compassion through the covering of Christ. When we do, he removes the weight of our sin. What a beautiful gift to us, and what a beautiful gift for others when we do the same.

Redeemer, you are full of merciful kindness toward us. Thank you for providing a way to complete forgiveness in your sacrifice. I come to you, Jesus, with all my shame. Forgive me. By your grace, empower me to forgive others in the same generous way.

RETURNS OF INCREASE

"I tell you the truth, all those who have left houses,
brothers, sisters, mother, father, children, or farms for me
and for the Good News will get more than they left. Here
in this world they will have a hundred times more homes,
brothers, sisters, mothers, children, and fields."

MARK 10:29-30 NCV

The economics of God's kingdom don't add up in
human logic. For those who leave behind all they had,
a multiplication of blessing and restoration is promised.
In the family of God, we find ourselves at home even
as strangers in foreign lands. When we meet fellow
Christians, we find homes, brothers, sisters, mothers,
children, and fields to share.

When we step out into the great unknown of following
God's direction in our lives, he often shows us only a
step or two at a time. We can't know the wonders we will
experience, the people we will meet, or the cultures we
will learn from. There is tremendous beauty in traveling
and in getting to know others we may have never known
if we had stayed home. Have courage to follow the Lord,
for he sets the lonely in families.

Jesus, I choose to follow you no matter where you lead.
I trust you will bring me to community wherever I go.

AUTHORITY TO OVERCOME

"Look, I have given you the authority to trample on
snakes and scorpion and over all the power of the enemy;
nothing at all will harm you."
LUKE 10:19 CSB

Not only do we have the authority of Christ to be merciful,
but in his name, we have power over the enemy and every
harm he wields. Love is the force that overcomes. It was
the fueling passion of Jesus' life, and it can be ours too.

When we partner with Jesus, ministering to others in his
name, we have his authority. We can trample on snakes
and scorpions without being harmed. We can convey the
liberty of Christ's love to all who are tormented. We are
sons and daughters of the living God, and as such, we can
exercise the authority of our Father because he has given
it to us. Romans 12:21 says not to be overcome by evil, but
to overcome evil with good.

Powerful Jesus, I want to walk in the power of your ways,
your name, and your presence. Go with me, empower
me by your grace, and continue to use me for your
kingdom.

GOD'S HEART

"This is the will of him who sent me,
that I shall lose none of all those he has given me,
but raise them up at the last day."
JOHN 6:39 NIV

God's heart is that everyone would look to Jesus, God made flesh, and be saved. Jesus' life, ministry, and teachings are straight from the Father's heart. Jesus went on to say, "My Father's will is that everyone who looks to the Son and believes in him shall have eternal life, and I will raise them up at the last day" (vs. 40).

May we live for the bigger picture and not just what satisfies our little lives. Every piece plays a part. Every one of us is a unique organ in the Body of Christ. Working together, we go further than we do alone. We can join with God's heart by joining with others who love him, believe his truth, and further his kingdom through practical acts of mercy and encouragement.

Jesus, thank you for your love that breaks barriers and unifies rather than divides. I am part of a big family of believers; help me not lose sight of that fact.

PRACTICAL PERSISTENCE

"If you keep my commands, you will remain in my love,
just as I have kept my Father's commands
and remain in his love."
JOHN 15:10 NKJV

How do we remain in the love of Christ? He makes it simple for us: keep his commands. We reveal what we truly believe by how we choose to live. When we keep the commands of Christ, it shows we value the truth and power of his ministry. When we make excuses for why we don't, it reveals we trust ourselves, or the ways of this world, more than the love of Christ.

Are there barriers or excuses you have allowed to keep you from remaining in the love of Christ? Which of his commands do not sit well with you? Which do you refuse to abide by? Take this opportunity to invite the Lord to correct what is out of alignment with his values. Are you willing to submit to his leadership?

Jesus, I come to you with a humble heart. Show me where I have allowed popular opinion or my own stubbornness to keep me from remaining in your love. Bring it all to the light and keep me in your love.

OVERFLOWING JOY

"These things I have spoken to you so that My joy may be
in you, and that your joy may be made full."
JOHN 15:11 NASB

Jesus' love was continually nourished and empowered
because he lived in alignment with the Father's love.
In the same way, when we remain in the love of Christ
by following his commands, we are nourished and
empowered to continue. Jesus spoke these things so our
joy would overflow.

Jesus does not give empty promises. He found joy in
unhindered fellowship with his Father, and that joy is ours
through him. We have been invited into the unbroken,
intimate fellowship of pure acceptance, love, and peace
that fueled Christ's passion even to death. May we find
our joy in the communion we have with Father, Son, and
Spirit, and may our delight grow with each encounter.

Jesus, thank you for the power of your love that makes
a way for me to enter into full fellowship with the
Father. Being yours is more than knowing about you; it
is knowing you and being known by you. Thank you for
the joy of this beautiful companionship.

WHEN TO SURRENDER

Pilate asked him, "Are you the King of the Jews?"
And he answered him, "You have said so."
MARK 15:2 ESV

Jesus didn't deny Pilate's question. He didn't deflect. He also didn't shout from the rooftops, "I am the King of the Jews!" He replied with a simple, "You have said so." It was enough to rile up the presiding priests. Pilate practically pleaded with Jesus to respond to the accusations of the priests, but he did not. He offered no defense. Jesus did not plead for his life, nor did he deny the priests' charges. Jesus did not need to defend himself because he already had the greatest advocate.

Are we willing to lay down our defenses and let God be our advocate even when we are unfairly accused? Jesus was as innocent as they come, yet he did not fight what he knew was going to happen. May we recognize when fighting is not the answer and trust God no matter what happens.

Jesus, give me courage to not rush to defend myself when others accuse me of acts I am not guilty of. I know you will be my advocate and the truth will be seen in time. I trust you.

MOTIVES

"Examine your motives to make sure you're not
showing off when you do your good deeds,
only to be admired by others; otherwise,
you will lose the reward of your heavenly Father."

MATTHEW 6:1 TPT

Jesus advised us to examine the motives of our hearts
when we are doing good deeds. Are we doing them for
the recognition of others, or do we serve because we
are spiritually compelled to do so? Those who give to be
admired will not follow through when no one is looking.

Integrity keeps us honest. It keeps us faithful. It keeps us
living by our guiding values because we believe in them
and not because we think they are the popular thing to
do. There is no need to show off, but there is a need to
keep showing up when it matters.

Heavenly Father, keep my heart pure in the values of
your kingdom. When I start to care more about what
others think rather than what is right, I know I have
lost my way. Lead me back to you, Lord.

THE POWER OF PEACE

"Why are you fearful, O you of little faith?"
Then He arose and rebuked the winds and the sea,
and there was a great calm.
MATTHEW 8:26 NKJV

We weren't in the boat when this storm was raging, but we know the disciples were scared for their lives. They were astonished when they saw Jesus sleeping through the whole thing. This wasn't a raincloud; it was a squall. Still, Jesus' response when they woke him up was basically, "What's your problem? Why are you scared?"

Depending on the situation, it can take more than a little pep talk to calm us down. Fortunately, Jesus is the Prince of Peace. He offers us the power of his peace through the fellowship of faith. Let's trust Jesus to keep us in perfect peace as we look to him. There is more calm in his presence than we can find on our own.

Prince of Peace, I look to you in times of calm and when the storms of life are raging. May your perfect peace settle my heart, mind, and soul in your presence. I trust you.

STRANGE REQUESTS

"Go into that village over there," he told them. "As soon as you enter it, you will see a young donkey tied there that no one has ever ridden. Untie it and bring it here."

MARK 11:2 NLT

Have you ever felt led to do something that didn't quite make sense to you? Did you follow through on it, or did you decide to ignore the nudge? When we follow Jesus, he will sometimes ask things of us that are above our understanding. We may not always know the reasons, but we can trust his leadership.

How can you know if it's God's guidance or your own thoughts? Truthfully, you won't always know. Test it according to the character of God. If it requires breaking a godly law, harming others, or giving in to fear, it's likely not the voice of God. Even in today's reading, there was a promise of return to the owner of the donkey. As you get to know the nature of God, you will know what to trust and what to let go of.

Jesus, I want to step out in faith as you speak to me. I know the best way to recognize your voice is to know your heart and your nature. I want to know you more, Lord.

POWERFUL FORGIVENESS

"Forgive us for our sins, because we forgive
everyone who has done wrong to us.
And do not cause us to be tempted."
Luke 11:4 NCV

God does not tempt us. In fact, James 1:13 says, "Evil
cannot tempt God, and God himself does not tempt
anyone." Not anyone. When we are tempted, evil desire
leads us and traps us. Not every desire is evil, and not
every evil is a desire. When we do sin, God is gracious to
forgive us when we come to him.

May we offer forgiveness as freely as we hope to receive it.
When we do this, we have no need to worry whether God
will offer us his mercy. As recipients of his generous love,
why would we withhold this same power from even those
who wrong us? When we let go of the need for revenge,
we free ourselves as much as we free them in the process.
The power of forgiveness is beautiful.

Merciful One, sometimes I am tempted to withhold
forgiveness even while knowing you have forgiven me. I
don't want to be ungrateful. Help me forgive even when
it's difficult, and may your justice roll like a mighty river
outside of my control.

LOVING LEADER

"When he has brought all his own outside,
he goes ahead of them. The sheep follow him
because they know his voice."
JOHN 10:4 CSB

Jesus is a perfect shepherd. He doesn't lose track of any that belong to him. He spends time with us, so we get to know his voice. We see his nature through accounts given in the gospels and from the letters his apostles wrote later. Knowing what he is like, we follow him willingly. He is a good leader who loves us.

Wherever we go in life, Jesus has already gone ahead of us. He knows every stone and obstacle in our path. As we listen to him, we learn where to avoid stepping and where we can confidently put our feet. He is watchful as he leads us into the unknown that is known to him. Let's follow Christ, our good shepherd and faithful friend.

Shepherd of my soul, I listen for your voice today.
Though the details of the future are unknown to me,
you already know. Lead me in your love, and I will follow.

KIND ACCOUNTABILITY

"If your brother or sister sins, go and point out their fault,
just between the two of you. If they listen to you,
you have won them over."
MATTHEW 18:15 NIV

When someone is causing pain through their choices, it's appropriate to confront them. Making others aware of ways they are harming others is an act of love. Perhaps you are holding a grudge against someone for something they thoughtlessly did that deeply affected you. Maybe you can think of someone you are concerned for because of their choices.

In both cases, the best course of action is as Jesus instructed. Go to them, alone, and lay out your case. Don't forget to listen to their response. Whether or not they receive it, a loving appeal has been made. This is how it must begin instead of gossiping with others or cutting them off without warning. Asserting yourself may feel uncomfortable, but it is as loving an act for yourself as it is for them.

Jesus, thank you for the kindness you use when dealing with my faults. May I be as kind and generous especially when first confronting conflict. Help me to be bold as well as kind.

NEW IDENTITY

"I also say to you that you are Peter,
and upon this rock I will build My church;
and the gates of Hades will not overpower it."
MATTHEW 16:18 NASB

Peter was a beloved disciple of Jesus. He was the first to say Jesus was the Messiah, and he was passionate in his devotion. While all this was true, Peter was not perfect. He spoke out of turn. He denied knowing Jesus on the night he was arrested. He said he would stick with Jesus until the end, but he didn't.

Even so, Jesus loved Peter, forgave him, and used his service. He told Peter, the man who would deny him, that he was the rock Jesus would build his church upon. Jesus can do far more with us than we could imagine accomplishing alone. Why wouldn't we submit our lives to him? He is the one who redeems, restores, and resurrects dead things to life again. He gives us a new name and a new identity. Those who belong to him are led into the abundance of his kingdom.

King Jesus, my life is yours. Give me a new name that reminds me of my true identity as your child. Have your way in my life, Lord.

LASTING GLORY

"Do you see these great buildings?
There will not be left here one stone upon another
that will not be thrown down."
MARK 13:2 ESV

Think about the last time you were impressed by someone
or something. What stood out to you? When Jesus was
walking through Jerusalem with his disciples, they were
impressed by the grandeur of the buildings surrounding
them. Though the temple was a sight to behold, Jesus told
them it would not stand.

Through the lens of history, we know the temple was
destroyed years later, but there is no need to mourn the
toppling of a building. The kingdom of Christ stands
through all ages, and no one can destroy it. Our hope is
not in an earthly dwelling—not even one dedicated to
God. It is in Christ himself. In him, we find lasting glory.

Lord of Glory, there is no one like you. There are no
secrets you can't see. I want to trust you more than I do
the systems of this world. Set my eyes on your eternal
kingdom when the governments of this world shake
and shatter.

NATURE CRIES OUT

"Listen to me. If my followers were silenced,
the very stones would break forth with praises!"
LUKE 19:40 TPT

Jesus' disciples had burst out in praises, quoting Psalm
118:26: "Highest praises to God for the one who comes as
King in the name of the Lord! Heaven's peace and glory
from the highest realm now comes to us!" In response,
some of the Jewish religious leaders warned Jesus to stop
his disciples from saying these things.

Today's verse was Jesus' response to that threat. He
claimed the rocks would cry out with praise if tongues
were silenced. The people had just witnessed mighty
wonders of power, and their response was to worship God.
Let's not inhibit our praises, for if we do, the stones will cry
out in our place.

Mighty Jesus, when you create miracles in my life,
what can I do but praise you? I will not stop myself
from showing the ecstatic joy rising within me. You are
wonderful and worthy to be praised!

FULL RESTORATION

"O Father, glorify Me together with Yourself, with the glory
which I had with You before the world was."
JOHN 17:5 NKJV

When Jesus reached the end of his ministry, he prayed. He
recognized the work he had been sent to do was largely
finished. It was time for him to return to the Father. In this
prayer, Jesus prayed he would be glorified so the Father
would also be glorified.

The Father revealed the glory of Jesus through his death
on the cross, the empty tomb that could not hold him, and
his ascension into heaven, but this was not all. The later
outpouring of the Holy Spirit would also be a testimony
of the Son's glory. The Son of God was fully restored to
his magnificence when his purpose on the earth was
completed, but he is still living and active in this world.
Now, his majesty is no longer hidden by his humanity. He
is glorified, and we will also be glorified in him.

**Son of God, your restoration is my hope. Every glimpse
of your glory in this earth and in my life is a tendril of joy
that teases the future beauty of my own restoration in
your glorious kingdom. Thank you for this hope.**

RELIEVING SUPPORT

"My soul is crushed with grief to the point of death.
Stay here and keep watch with me."
MATTHEW 26:38 NLT

Jesus felt the weight of his bone-crushing grief. He knew what awaited him in the coming hours, and while he prayed, he turned to his disciples for comfort too. Though grief is a lonely and heavy weight to bear, there is some relief in having others sit with us in it. However, we can't pass our sorrow to someone else to carry. We must go through it.

Close and trusted friends are an unrivaled gift. Their presence can give us a modicum of hope in a dark night of the soul. Have you ever "kept watch" with a friend who was in so much pain that they didn't know how they would handle it? It does not require knowing what to do or how to fix it. Your very presence can make a powerful difference between utter despair and holding on through the storm.

Jesus, strange as it may sound, I am relieved you experienced the depths of grief. I can relate to you in it. Thank you for the power of presence and support. Give me courage to ask for help when I need it and to show up when others need me.

AWAKE

> After Jesus prayed a third time, he went back to his followers and said to them, "Are you still sleeping and resting? That's enough. The time has come for the Son of Man to be handed over to sinful people."
>
> MARK 14:41 NCV

After Jesus asked his disciples to keep watch with him, they kept falling asleep. Jesus left them twice more to go pray. In his overwhelming grief, not one of his disciples stayed up to keep watch with him. They couldn't keep their eyes open.

When Jesus asks us to keep watch with him, what is our response? Do we take him seriously and lay down our needs when he has pressing matters, or do we prioritize our rest? This is not a one-size-fits-all situation. Sometimes, Jesus will ask us to deny what we want in support of his purposes. Other times, he will move with us in what we choose. Knowing the timing and importance of a response is more practice than perfection. Let's join our hearts to the Lord's and be moved by what moves him.

Jesus, I don't want to dismiss your feelings or purposes. You are full of emotions just as I am. I'm awake now, Lord. Tell me what's on your heart and what you want me to do.

CALLED BY NAME

"The gatekeeper opens it for him, and the sheep hear his voice. He calls his own sheep by name and leads them out."
JOHN 10:3 CSB

Jesus Christ, the one who was, is, and is yet to come, knows your name. He calls to you and beckons to follow him. He knows every hair on your head, the silly things that light up your eyes, the songs that make you get up and dance. He knows you better than any friend or family member, and he delights in you.

If you feel hesitant to trust him today, take that first step toward him. Let his love guide you and his kindness draw you nearer. Don't be afraid to look at the whole of who he is. He is an open book, and he will not abandon you in your questions. Look into the face of pure mercy and let him shower you with his praises. You are his, you belong to him, and he will lead you out.

Jesus, I respond to your call today. I take a step of faith knowing you will meet me. I trust you to guide me in kindness, care, and wisdom.

WITNESSES

"You are witnesses of these things."
LUKE 24:48 NIV

When God works in our lives, we become witnesses of
his mighty power. We each have a story to tell of God's
greatness. We can share the unique ways his mercy
has transformed us. Do we forget what he did at first?
Remember the pure love and devotion of those early days.
Recall the beauty of God's love and the refreshing power
of his presence.

If this all feels unfamiliar, ask the Lord to reveal practical
ways he has showed up for you. Write down what comes
to mind. As you look over your history with God, no matter
how long or short it's been, let the Spirit of God bring to
mind specific ways he answered your prayers. As he does,
give thanks, for you are a witness of his power.

Powerful Jesus, as I think over my journey with you,
reveal any answers to prayer I have forgotten about.
Remind me of the ways you have met me with your
marvelous mercy so I may thank you again and share
my story with others.

YIELD TO HIS HEART

"Is it not lawful for me to do what I want with what is my own? Or is your eye envious because I am generous?"
MATTHEW 20:15 NASB

We will never truly understand God's mercy and why he does what he does until we understand his heart. He welcomes the stranger as warmly as he welcomes a close friend. He offers the same mercy to all who come to him.

This goes against the narrative that we earn God's love. We just can't. No matter how little or long we serve the Lord, we are offered the same generous gift for our service: full adoption as children of God. We each receive inheritance as his daughters and sons. May we remain humble in his love and join with his heart in how we treat others.

Heavenly Father, in a world of limitations and limited resources, it's difficult to imagine there is enough for everyone. Break the scarcity mindset I have lived in as I yield to your heart. I want to better understand the depths of your love and mercy.

SEPTEMBER

"Don't worry about tomorrow,
for tomorrow will bring its
own worries. Today's trouble
is enough for today."

MATTHEW 6:34 NLT

SPIRIT OF TRUTH

"When the Spirit of truth comes, he will guide you into all the truth, for he will not speak on his own authority, but whatever he hears he will speak, and he will declare to you the things that are to come."
JOHN 16:13 ESV

The Spirit of truth is none other than the Holy Spirit, and all he reveals comes from the Father. Just as Jesus did what he saw the Father doing, the Spirit only says what he hears the Father saying. We can trust the Spirit to reveal the heart of God and the truth of his kingdom.

It's a lot of pressure to feel we must retain every bit of knowledge we learn. A student learns many things, but they don't remember them all. Apprentices lean on the knowledge and example of a master in the trade. We are like apprentices of Jesus, and the Holy Spirit helps us in real time to lead us to the truth. The pressure of perfection is off, and we can learn as he leads.

Spirit of truth, thank you for your help in all things. I don't have to lean on my limited understanding. You teach me as I look to you, and you help me correct my mistakes along the way. Please teach me something new today.

THE INVITATION

"On the day the festivities were set to begin,
he sent his servants to summon all the invited guests,
but they chose not to come."
MATTHEW 22:3 TPT

Could you imagine being invited to a king's lavish wedding and refusing to go? What better thing could you do with your time? Those who were invited by the king in this parable had excuses for why they decided not to come, and their choices seemed right to them.

The royal invitation of Christ is offered to us. Do we avoid coming to his bountiful, joyous banquet because we are too busy with our lives? We may have excuses, but in light of what we miss out on, they are never worth it. Today, let's look at our priorities from the kingdom's view rather than the world's. There is more abundance waiting for us than we realize as we enter into fellowship with Christ.

Lord Jesus, I don't want to make any more excuses for why I can't fully submit to you. My life is yours. Have your way. You are worth it.

THE TIME HAS COME

"He sent other servants to tell them, 'The feast has been prepared. The bulls and fattened cattle have been killed, and everything is ready. Come to the banquet!'"

MATTHEW 22:4 NLT

Not giving up after one round of invitations, the king in Jesus' story sent his servants to tell those invited that the feast was ready. This was their last chance; it was time to come to the banquet. When we hear the invitation of Christ, do we come to him? Or do we hesitate?

2 Corinthians 6:2 says, "Indeed, the 'right time' is now. Today is the day of salvation." Will we ignore the marvelous gift of God's kindness, or will we embrace it with joy? There is more awaiting us in the bounty of God's kingdom than we leave behind. May we heed his call and come to his feast today.

King Jesus, I answer your call and come to the banquet of your love. You have spared no expense, and nothing I leave behind can compare to the priceless gift of being welcomed to your table as an honored guest.

EVERYONE WELCOME

"The king said to his servants, 'The wedding feast is ready.
I invited those people, but they were not worthy to come.
So go to the street corners and invite everyone you find
to come to my feast.'"

MATTHEW 22:8-9 NCV

What made the wedding feast attendants worthy?
Nothing more than accepting the invitation and following
through. We enter Christ's kingdom the same way. We
are not worthy because of where we live, what name we
go by, or anything other than our willingness to come
to Christ. We take him up on his invitation and enter the
banquet hall of his goodness.

Notice that the king instructed his servants to go to
the street corners, the place where all different types of
people gather, and invite everyone they found. Just as
Christ does not discriminate with his invitation, we are to
live openheartedly with all kinds of people.

Jesus, I don't know where I picked up the idea that you
are selective in your invitation. There are no limits in or
to your love. Please make my heart more like yours.

A FEW REPLY

"Many are invited,
but few are chosen."
MATTHEW 22:14 CSB

Though many are called to follow Christ, few choose to do it. The ones who do are chosen, not because they are special, but because they are willing. Have you answered the call of Christ to follow him? Have you surrendered to his kingdom ways? Whether you have walked with him for an hour or a lifetime, his love reaches out to you in the same abundant measure.

Think of the context of this verse; it's within the story of an invitation to a glorious wedding feast. Those who choose to not accept the invitation and come to the banquet are the ones missing out. May we be quick in our response to Jesus' invitation, for what awaits us is bounteous, beautiful, and fulfilling.

Lord Jesus, I would rather follow you than try to make my own way in this life. Keep my eyes fixed on your kingdom so I don't get distracted. I come to you, and I rely on your help to take every step of this journey.

PROVISIONS FOR TODAY

"Give us each day our daily bread."
Luke 11:3 NIV

Written within the Lord's prayer is a simple request: "Give us each day our daily bread." This is not just about what we eat; it speaks to the provision for all we need. We need water, food, and rest to live. When we ask God to give us our sustenance for each day, we declare our trust in his lordship over our lives and in his ability to provide.

Instead of running with every thought that crosses your mind, take a few moments in silence to ground yourself in the present love of Christ. Take a few deep breaths, feel your body ease and your mind quiet, and take some time to pray the Lord's prayer over your day. As you do, give God the things you can't control and the worries that keep you distracted. He will provide all you need according to his grace.

Gracious Jesus, thank you for teaching us how to turn our hearts to the Father and trust in his provision. I join with your heart and pray as you taught your disciples to pray.

DEEP LOVE

"For God so loved the world that He gave His only
begotten Son, that whoever believes in Him
should not perish but have everlasting life."
JOHN 3:16 NKJV

God showed his great love for us in sending his Son. Jesus,
the Lamb of God, was the all-sufficient sacrifice for all
creation. Hebrews 10:10 puts it this way: "We have been
sanctified through the offering of the body of Jesus Christ
once for all." It is through this offering that, as Paul said,
"There is now no condemnation to those who are in
Christ Jesus" (Romans 8:1).

Our freedom is found in Christ's sacrifice. As we live under
the banner of his strong love, submitted to his ways,
we show our true belief; as true believers, we have the
promise of everlasting life. Why did God do any of this?
He did it for love. Our response to his love is to love.

Jesus, thank you for revealing the deep love of the
Father's heart through your teachings, lifestyle, death,
and triumphant resurrection. May the revelation of this
powerful love go deeper in me as your Spirit reveals it.

OPEN THRESHOLD

"I am the door; if anyone enters through Me, he will
be saved, and will go in and out and find pasture."
JOHN 10:9 NASB

Jesus had just been talking about the kind shepherd
whose sheep know his voice. His sheep follow his voice
and don't follow strangers because they know the
difference. Here, Jesus says he is the gate for the flock to
enter through. When they come through him, his people
find satisfaction, life, and freedom. They find peace.

Jesus is our gateway; he is the door. In him, we find the
abundant satisfaction of his pasture. Through him, we find
rest in his kingdom. As we rely on him, knowing his voice
and following him as he leads, our confidence is in his care
of us. He will not leave us, and he will never abandon us.
He is the kind and good shepherd whom we trust.

Good Shepherd, I trust your care of me. May I know your
voice more and more as I follow you. Your character
doesn't change, and you don't trick your people. I trust
you, and I find rest under your watchful gaze.

ABUNDANT LIFE

"The thief comes only to steal and kill and destroy.
I came that they may have life and have it abundantly."
JOHN 10:10 ESV

A thief concentrates on one thing: to steal. To follow through on that, they may also destroy and kill to be successful. Jesus is not a thief, nor is the Father he represents. He came to bring abundant life, more than we could imagine or expect. He brings overflowing life to us.

Through his Spirit, we experience the abundance of Christ's love for us. There is more generosity in his heart than we can fathom. May we submit to his leadership, for he guards us from the enemy, and he will not let us be stolen from his flock. We now live by faith in the Son of God who loved us and gave himself for us. We are empowered by Christ's life in us. What a glorious and abundant grace.

Lord Jesus, I can't begin to thank you for the power of your love in my life, but I will try. Infuse my life with the Spirit's powerful, generous love as I yield my heart to you today.

GATHER IN HIS NAME

"Wherever two or three come together in honor of my name, I am right there with them!"
MATTHEW 18:20 TPT

There is power in the name of Jesus Christ. Philippians 2:10 says, "The authority of the name of Jesus causes every knee to bow in reverence! Everything and everyone will one day submit to this name." We can experience this great power in personal time with the Lord and even more when we gather in his name.

There is encouragement for our souls in fellowship with other believers. When we come together to pray with unity, the Spirit of God moves, and Christ is there with us. There is no better place to lift up our hearts in prayer than with those whose hearts are woven together in love. Let's pray together for the breakthroughs we long to receive. God is with us when we do.

Jesus, thank you for the promise of your presence as we join together in your name. Help me find people to pray with and for. Please bring encouragement and breakthrough for each of us.

HE GETS IT

At three o'clock Jesus called out with a loud voice,
"Eloi, Eloi, lema sabachthani?" which means
"My God, my God, why have you abandoned me?"
MARK 15:34 NLT

There is nothing Jesus doesn't understand of the human experience—not even abandonment. When Christ was on the cross, he yelled, "My God, my God, why have you abandoned me?" He felt utterly lost and alone in this desperate moment. This was not hyperbole on his part. He felt it to his core.

Have you ever gone through a loss so great you felt as Jesus did? Even as you wonder how God could allow something so awful to happen, perhaps you can find solace in the solidarity of Jesus. He truly understands. Let his humanity encourage you to press further into his heart and receive the comfort he offers. He knows what you are going through, beloved. He knows.

Jesus, I know I can't escape the agony of grief. I know you have felt that agony too. Minister to me and comfort me in my pain. You are my healer, Savior, and deliverer.

WORTH IT

"It is worthless to have the whole world
if they themselves are destroyed or lost."
LUKE 9:25 NCV

Even if you gained great wealth and everything you could dream of attaining, it would do nothing for the state of your soul. You can't buy yourself peace. You can't use your resources to gain the wisdom of God. It is freely given to all who seek it. Jesus welcomes all who come to him whether poor or rich. Your wealth does not give you greater access. In fact, it will inhibit you if you love money more than you love Christ.

Most of us will not be rich. Many of us scrape to get by; some live comfortably. The point isn't how much money we earn. How do we live? Do we compromise our morals or the values of God's kingdom in favor of getting ahead? As Jesus said, it's not worth it if you lose your soul in the process. Follow him, guard your heart and mind in integrity, and give generously. When he asks you to lay down your comfort and ambitions, can you do it?

Jesus, I don't want to gain power but lose myself along the way. Make me wise with my resources and generous with what I have.

SHIFTED EXPECTATIONS

"You will be hated by everyone because of my name,
but the one who endures to the end will be saved."
MARK 13:13 CSB

What is your view of this life? Do you expect it to be
smooth and easy? Perhaps you have had a pretty seamless
life so far. Maybe the opposite is true; you've experienced
many trials and hiccups along the way. You may fall
somewhere in the middle. Life isn't about how easy it is;
it's about the fruit that grows from it.

Jesus warned his disciples they would be hated because
of him. Some would despise them simply because of
their association. Endurance is a fruit of the Spirit because
it is necessary to a life of faith. Whatever troubles you
have today, no matter who has turned on you, may
perseverance keep you going. You never go it alone. You
are with Christ and all his followers.

Patient Lord, I don't want to suffer, but I also know I can't
avoid pain in this life. I choose to follow you because you
are better than anyone I know. I know you won't leave
me when life gets hard. Help me, Lord.

NEW FAMILY

When Jesus saw his mother there, and the disciple whom he loved standing nearby, he said to her, "Woman, here is your son," and to the disciple, "Here is your mother." From that time on, this disciple took her into his home.
JOHN 19:26-27 NIV

When Jesus was dying on the cross, he saw his mother and his friend, John, nearby. He knew their grief was great. Although no one could replace him in their lives, he knew they needed each other. He spent some of his last energy encouraging them to find solace in taking care of each other.

When loss rips through our lives and leaves a gaping hole in its wake, Jesus offers us the comfort of others. No one can replace our lost fathers, mothers, siblings, or friends, but we can find comfort in our shared loss. We can care for each other the way Christ cares for us. It's a beautiful reflection of the Spirit's work in us.

Kind Jesus, your love sees me in my grief and offers me comfort not only in your Spirit but in human relationships too. Thank you for that. In deep grief, may we bring relief to each other through friendship that feels like family.

JUSTICE IS COMING

"Shall God not avenge His own elect who cry out day and night to Him, though He bears long with them?"
LUKE 18:7 NKJV

God answers the requests of the persistent. He will not ignore the cries of the suffering. Though it feels like he's taking his sweet time, he is with us in our grief. Justice will roll, and he will grant it to all who cry out to him day and night.

Every prayer you utter is recorded and remembered by God; he doesn't forget a single one. Your persistence will pay off in the end. He will answer your prayers, and he will come to your aid when you need it. Don't grow discouraged; let your longing keep you praying, seeking, and advocating for others who also need God's intervention. He hears and knows, and he will answer.

God of Justice, I trust you will not let the powerful abuse their power forever. Bring justice, Lord, and let it roll like a mighty river. I won't stop praying for your kingdom to come and your will to be done.

GOD'S PURPOSES

"This is the will of My Father, that everyone who sees
the Son and believes in Him will have eternal life,
and I Myself will raise him up on the last day."
JOHN 6:40 NASB

The longing of the Father is for everyone to experience
eternal life in his kingdom. Jesus was sent so we might
know, love, and embrace him as the way, the truth, and
the life. Jesus revealed the heart of the Father in his
ministry. Human logic had muddled the understanding
of God's heart through history; the gospel was made to
be simple and accessible to all who believe.

We don't need to go to seminary to serve God. We don't
need to run in the right circles to minister. Everyone who
believes and embraces the ways of Christ is empowered
by the Spirit of God. Our faith comes from God; he always
initiates. We accept his invitation, and we get to partner
with his purposes as we follow him.

Jesus, you are my Savior. You are the only way to truly
know the Father. Thank you for loving me first, paving a
way to the kingdom, and inviting me to join you there.

THE GOLDEN RULE

"Whatever you wish that others would do to you,
do also to them, for this is the Law and the Prophets."
MATTHEW 7:12 ESV

The law of love is simple: love God with your whole being and treat others in the same way you want them to treat you. To say that it is simple, however, does not devalue the cost. Though simple, it's not easy to choose to live this way.

We need the grace of God to empower us. We need the mercy of God to transform us. We need grateful hearts that recognize the power of God's love in our lives. We need Jesus, and we need the Spirit to help us. The directive is clear. The law and the prophets can be summed up in the golden rule. We can't follow Christ and ignore our responsibility to reflect his love to others.

Lord Jesus, thank you for the power of your love; it breaks through my selfish ways. I choose to be practical in love toward others when I would rather stay comfortable. Help me live the way you instructed. I need the power of your grace.

EVERY PROPHECY FULFILLED

"Everything that has happened fulfills what was prophesied of me. Christ, the Messiah, was destined to suffer and rise from the dead on the third day."
LUKE 24:46 TPT

Even at the beginning, Jesus' life was filled with the prophetic fulfillment required for the Messiah. The prophecies that foretold his coming included complex details: where he was born, the donkey he rode when entering Jerusalem, and many more. Every detail was covered. He did not forget a single one.

This is how God works even now. We can take hope in this fact. The God of the universe is also the God of the details. He will not overlook what he has promised, and we will see the glory of the Lord in the land of the living. We will see the goodness of God play out in our lives.

Lord of all, you don't miss any miniscule detail. I'm grateful to be yours and rest in the faithfulness of your character. Give me eyes to see where you are fulfilling my prayers both old and new. I give you thanks for all you have and will continue to do.

FOOD FOR THOUGHT

"Beware of these teachers of religious law! For they like to parade around in flowing robes and receive respectful greetings as they walk in the marketplaces."

MARK 12:38 NLT

There is no shortage of religious teachers and figures in our society, but just because they claim to know God doesn't mean they do. The teachers of the religious law in Jesus' day were supposed to be experts in God's identity, yet they didn't recognize him when he stood before them.

Just because someone has studied theology or created a platform for themselves in the name of Christ does not mean they value the actual teachings and ways of Jesus Christ. Many people parade around their titles, looking for recognition and respect, while not doing the least of what Christ says we should. Don't be impressed by degrees, power, or the presentation of a person. Be impressed by the way they lay their lives down to show mercy, promote peace, and stand for justice.

Jesus, knowing you is not about prestige, power, or worldly respect. It's about living out the love you so lavishly pour out over us. Make me discerning; help me stay true to your Word.

PRAY FOR STRENGTH

"Stay awake and pray for strength against temptation.
The spirit wants to do what is right, but the body is weak."
MATTHEW 26:41 NCV

When Jesus was in the garden of Gethsemane, he asked his disciples to keep watch with him. Instead, they fell asleep. Though our spirits are eager to do the right thing, our humanity is weak. We must rely on the grace and strength of God to help when we grow weary. We must stay alert and pray for the energy we need to withstand temptation.

Are there areas of your life where you feel this to your core? Perhaps you keep going back to something even though you know it's not good for you. Instead of being pulled back in without a fight, stay alert to your patterns, pray for strength, and ask the Lord for help.

Lord, I need your help to stay alert in areas where it's easy for me to drift. Awaken my heart in the strength of your Spirit's power. I want to do the right thing and not the easy thing.

HUMBLE HEARTS

"Will he thank the servant because he did what he was told to do? So you also, when you have done everything you were told to do, should say, 'We are unworthy servants; we have only done our duty.'"
LUKE 17:9-10 NIV

How humbly we serve the Lord may show up as persistence in our lives. When we keep our hearts soft and teachable, we are ready for whatever God requires of us. When we submit to his ways, we take them on as our own. We follow him because he is trustworthy, kind, and wise. There is no better way to go about life.

Jesus is the example of perfect humble. Philippians 2 says it well: "Have the same mindset as Christ Jesus: who, being in very nature God, did not consider equality with God something to be used to his own advantage; rather, he made himself nothing by taking the very nature of a servant…he humbled himself by becoming obedient to death" (vs. 5-8). If this was how Jesus lived, how much more should we?

Jesus, I look to your example of servant-hearted humility as the ultimate encouragement to remain teachable, obedient, and open to you. Thank you.

POWERLESS APART

"Remain in me, and I in you. Just as a branch is unable
to produce fruit by itself unless it remains on the vine,
neither can you unless you remain in me."
JOHN 15:4 CSB

Abiding in Christ is the most powerful decision we can make, so what does it mean to abide? We submit our hearts, yield to his ways by adopting them as our own, and look to Christ for our needs. He is our provider, strength, and passion.

Let us find our strength in the Spirit-to-spirit fellowship we have access to through Christ. As Proverbs 3:5 says, we must trust in the Lord with all our hearts and not lean on our understanding. When we acknowledge God in all our ways and submit to his leadership, he makes our paths straight. He is our ultimate source.

Jesus, you are the most powerful source in this world. Why should I try to light my own life when I can plug into you and remain connected to the greatest power source? I choose to abide in you today and every day.

LIKE LITTLE CHILDREN

"Unless you are converted and become as little children,
you will by no means enter the kingdom of heaven."
MATTHEW 18:3 NKJV

Childlike attributes are especially important to those who follow Christ. It's how we enter his kingdom. What does becoming little children look like? They are trusting, forgive easily, and constantly learn and look for guidance. They rely on the provision of their caregivers. They change their minds when presented with new information. They love easily and without restraint. They are honest.

What would you add to this list? Are there any attributes you can integrate into your faith walk? In all things, Christ helps those who ask him. As we become like little children before him, we get to share in the partnership of learning, growing, and trusting him.

Lord Jesus, I see specific ways I can grow in my childlike faith. Help me shed the layers of jaded mistrust I have learned in this world so I can wholly follow you.

THE LAST FIRST

"Many who are first will be last,
and the last, first."
MARK 10:31 NASB

Could you imagine running a race you had trained for, doing your very best, and when you get to the end, the medals are awarded to those who crossed the finish line last? It doesn't seem fair. Still, the Lord says those who struggle may be first in his kingdom and some who seem to have it together will be last.

We can't read people's hearts, but we can live with the awareness of God reading our hearts and not our accomplishments. That's what he weighs. Some people will face more difficulties than others, and this is not a formal accusation on their worth or their submission to Christ. Jesus is not a magic pill to make our problems disappear. However, he is with each of us who rely on him, and he will never abandon those who cry out to him.

Jesus, I trust that you, the Father, and the Spirit see each of us as we really are. Keep me from judging others based on their appearance and achievements. You look at the heart. Thank you for your generous grace.

A DIFFERENT WAY

"The kings and men of authority in this world rule oppressively over their subjects, claiming that they do it for the good of the people. They are obsessed with how others see them."
LUKE 22:25 TPT

Oppressive regimes do not only belong to nations under dictators. They are built into every society, and some hide it better than others. Authorities often rule with their own interests in mind and not those of the people. Power and greed corrupt the hearts of those who love status and wealth more than the people they trample to get there.

The kingdom of Christ does not work this way. Jesus was not concerned with how others perceived him. He did not change his ministry tactics when people started critiquing him. He had one focus: the will of the Father. May we follow in his footsteps and not the deceiving paths the world tries to lure us down. God's ways are always better.

King Jesus, I love that you spoke the truth to people in power. Still, you submitted yourself to the laws of the land. You did no wrong, yet you were still ridiculed. I want to value who you say I am more than anyone's opinion of me.

LEAD BY EXAMPLE

"Rather, let the greatest among you become as the youngest, and the leader as one who serves."
LUKE 22:26 ESV

Is our duty as followers of Christ to earn the good opinion of others or to live overflowing with acts of love? We spread the powerful gospel message when we submit ourselves as those who are here to serve others rather than to rule over them.

True, godly leadership is in how we serve others. It is not afraid to get down and dirty. It does not consider itself better than any person or task. It is patient, kind, and easily directed. Think of all the things 1 Corinthians 13 says about love. God is love, and Jesus is the incarnation of that love; how he leads reflects love. We can lead with the submission that love requires. It always protects, always trusts, always hopes, and always perseveres (vs. 7).

Merciful Jesus, thank you for the power of your servant leadership. I'm not above you, and I don't know better than you. I choose to follow your path of laid-down love.

UPSIDE–DOWN KINGDOM

"Who is more important, the one who sits at the table or the one who serves? The one who sits at the table, of course. But not here! For I am among you as one who serves."
LUKE 22:27 NLT

Jesus flipped the script of what a person's worth is weighed by. It is not by status, wealth, or beauty. It is not in the things this world values. It is not what we are told to long for, work toward, or judge others on. Worthy people are not found sitting at exclusive tables being waited on; they are the servants.

Jesus did not demand we become servants. He lived it for us, and his life is the example we follow. If all believers in Christ truly lived this way, our communities would look vastly different. Churches would not be exclusive gatherings instead but would serve in places where needs are the greatest. In light of this, how can we take a step toward being more Christlike?

Jesus, I've been caught up in the values of this world rather than the values of your kingdom. Forgive me for my folly. I choose to follow you in service and let you promote me rather than live for the favor of others.

NO MORE WAITING

Jesus said, "I am he—
I, the one talking to you."
JOHN 4:26 NCV

We must wait for many things in life. We can't will ourselves into growing up, and we can't immediately feast on the fruit of an orchard that has just been planted. But there is one thing we don't need to wait on: full fellowship with God through Christ. Christ is the Messiah, he has already come, and he has provided we need to come to the Father through him.

Let's not wait a moment longer to approach him. Let's not waste another second before we submit to him. He is worthy of our time, affection, and trust. He does not lead us into deserts without providing food and water to satisfy us. He is better than anything else we wait for, and he is the perfect fulfillment of all we long for. He is here now.

Jesus Christ, I come to you with an open and willing heart. Though I must wait on some things, I'm glad I don't have to wait a moment longer to know you, walk with you, and experience the lengths of your luxurious love. Thank you!

HIS CHOICE

Reaching out his hand, Jesus touched him, saying,
"I am willing; be made clean."
Immediately his leprosy was cleansed.
MATTHEW 8:3 CSB

The man with leprosy threw himself before Jesus and worshiped. He said, "Lord, if you choose, you can make me clean." Jesus did not hesitate with his response. "I do choose." How simple a statement, but how indescribably powerful it must have been to this man. The goodness of God was displayed in those three words: "I do choose."

If Jesus appeared to you in the flesh, what would you run to him and tell him? Would you ask him for something? The presence of God is with you now. Approach him, worship him, and pour out your heart to him. Listen for his response. He is near, and he will answer you, for he is full of power and goodness.

Healer, I come to you with a wide-open heart. I won't hold back a single request or prayer today. Meet me, hear me, and answer me. I am waiting on your response.

LESSONS IN TRUST

"When I broke the seven loaves for the four thousand,
how many basketfuls of pieces did you pick up?"
They answered, "Seven."
MARK 8:20 NIV

Every previous provision by God is a testament to his
faithfulness. We need not forget yesterday's miracles
because of today's worries. Our faith builds as we
recognize the goodness and trustworthiness of our God.

What has God done for you? Has he come through in
miraculous ways that felt profoundly simple at the time?
As you remember, let your soul fill with resolute hope.
What God has done before, he will do again. He provides
for the needs of his people. He rescues those who call on
him. He is faithful to do everything he promised and so
much more. Let's give him all worries, along with our trust.
He will not fail us.

Lord Jesus, thank you teaching patiently even though
you have every right not to. I am a slow learner, but you
don't give up on me. As I remember all you have done,
open my eyes to see what you are doing. As to what I
can't see, I choose to trust you.

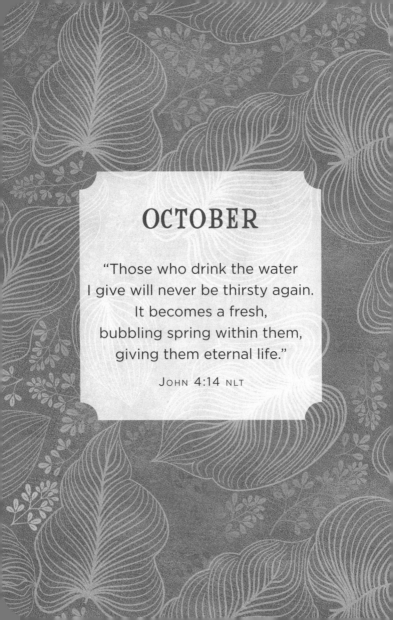

OCTOBER

"Those who drink the water
I give will never be thirsty again.
It becomes a fresh,
bubbling spring within them,
giving them eternal life."

JOHN 4:14 NLT

ABSOLUTE ASSURANCE

"Most assuredly, I say to you,
he who believes in Me has everlasting life."
JOHN 6:47 NKJV

How confident are you of your salvation? Do you doubt the power of God's mercy? If you believe in Christ and are submitted to his leadership over your life, you can redirect under his love, ask forgiveness when you have wronged someone, and change your behavior going forward. That's all by his power; you can rest assured.

If you believe Christ is the Son of God, you don't need to be perfect, for only he is the perfect sacrifice. You do need to yield to him. It's not enough to say you believe in him if it doesn't change your heart. Only you and God know what goes on in your heart. Look to him for assurance today and surrender to his love. It is a vast waterfall of goodness, kindness, and mercy.

Savior, there is no one like you in the universe. You are the way, the truth, and the life. I submit to your loving leadership, and I humble myself before you.

GRACE AND WISDOM

"Determine in your hearts not to prepare for your own defense. Simply speak with the words of wisdom that I will give you that moment, and none of your persecutors will be able to withstand the grace and wisdom that comes from your mouths."

LUKE 21:14-15 TPT

The Spirit of God will rise to meet you in the moments you need him most. You don't have to perfectly word your defense. The Spirit of grace and wisdom, the Holy Spirit, will give you the right words at the right moment.

When the Spirit speaks, the gracious wisdom of the kingdom of God comes forward. Its truth sets captives free and puts oppressors in their place. When you are persecuted for being true to the gospel of Christ, the Lord will be your defender. You will be able to testify to his mercy, power, and wisdom. Don't stay silent when the Lord calls you to speak, and don't rush to speak when he tells you to wait.

Gracious Jesus, I won't worry about what I will say to those who harass me. I know you will give me the right words, full of grace and wisdom, at the right time.

IMPORTANT COMMANDMENTS

He said to Him, "Which ones?" And Jesus said,
"you shall not commit murder; you shall not commit
adultery; you shall not steal; you shall not give false
testimony; honor your father and mother;
and you shall love your neighbor as yourself."
MATTHEW 19:18-19 NASB

When the rich young man asked which commandments he should keep, wondering about eternal life's requirements, Jesus responded with these. It's a high standard to keep—especially considering Jesus said even looking at someone with malice in your heart, wishing for their destruction, it is as good as murder.

No matter how hard we try to keep the commandments of the law, none of us can do it without flaw. We need Jesus. We need his mercy, grace, and power. We need humble hearts, quick repentance, and full submission. Jesus is the only one powerful enough to overcome sin and death and lead us into life everlasting.

Jesus, I will not ignore the wisdom of your truth which asks me to try my best. I also will not ignore how desperately I need your help to achieve even that! Thank you for the gracious gift of your salvation.

HONORED BY CHRIST

"Wherever the gospel is proclaimed in the whole world, what she has done will be told in memory of her."
MARK 14:9 ESV

When Mary poured expensive perfume over Jesus' feet, anointing them with oil and her tears, it was a precious act. Though others questioned why he would allow her to do such a thing, Jesus told them to back off. In fact, he didn't stop there; he said wherever the gospel is told around the world, her generous act will be told as well.

Jesus honored Mary even as she honored him. Will he not do the same for you? When you offer him your generous gift of worship, he welcomes it. It ministers to his heart, and he will honor you for it. Trust him to do it even if others don't understand you. He never mistakes your love.

Jesus, thank you for honoring your followers. You give honor where others seek to tear a person down. I won't hold back my worship from you. You know my heart, and you will receive what I offer. Thank you.

UNDER COVER

"You seem to be in a deep discussion about something.
What are you talking about, so sad and gloomy?"
LUKE 24:17 TPT

After Jesus died, his disciples were devastated. They were in deep grief and shock that Jesus was no longer with them. As two of these sad disciples were walking from Jerusalem to Emmaus, Jesus appeared to them, but they did not recognize him. This is where today's verse comes in. Jesus began a conversation with these men who knew him. He had prepared them for his death and resurrection, but they could not understand it. They were trying to make sense of it.

Jesus' interaction may seem callous if we don't understand his heart. He took the time to go through the prophecies spoken about himself to open their eyes to God's plan. Only after they parted did they realize he was Jesus. God can come to us in ways we don't recognize, but later, looking back, he is unmistakable.

Gracious Jesus, open my eyes to see you at work in my life. Give me ears to recognize your voice. You are who you say you are.

JOY WILL COME

"I tell you the truth, you will weep and mourn over what is going to happen to me, but the world will rejoice. You will grieve, but your grief will suddenly turn to wonderful joy."
JOHN 16:20 NLT

Reading through the gospels, it's astounding how many times Jesus warned his listeners of his death. Jesus wouldn't escape the inevitable suffering that was his to experience, but he promised the disciples' grief would turn to wonderful joy. We see this clearly through the lens of history. He rose from the grave and appeared to his disciples. Their crushing grief quickly turned to rejoicing.

We can't escape heartbreaking pain either. The pain of our losses may not ease as quickly as we like, but God promises joy will come. Isaiah 61:3 says, "To all who mourn…he will give a crown of beauty for ashes, a joyous blessing instead of mourning, festive praise instead of despair." He will do this for all who believe in him. Joy will come, and praise will replace our despair. Hold on if you haven't experienced it yet.

Generous Jesus, I look forward to the promised relief of your joy. Until that day, relieve my pain with the close comfort of your presence.

EVERYTHING MADE NEW

> The One who was sitting on the throne said, "Look! I am making everything new!" Then he said, "Write this, because these words are true and can be trusted."
>
> REVELATION 21:5 NCV

Jesus will make everything new including each of us. It's what his mercy does. He does not simply spruce up or repair us; he makes us completely new in his great love. Whatever has worn out and needs the merciful power of Christ will receive it as we submit it to him.

We can offer him access to all we are and all we have. He is trustworthy and true. God is not like humans who lie or change their minds. "What he says he will do, he does. What he promises, he makes come true" (Numbers 23:19). This is the God who says, "Look! I am making everything new!" Everything includes you.

Wonderful Jesus, I'm grateful for the power of your presence in my life. Shine on me and make me new in the life-giving light of your love today.

BLESSINGS OF GIVING

In every way I have shown you that it is necessary to help the weak by laboring like this and to remember the words of the Lord Jesus, because he said, "It is more blessed to give than to receive."

ACTS 20:35 CSB

We are blessed when we receive but even more blessed when we give. Before this statement, Paul explained how he worked for his own needs and the needs of those who were with him. It's an act of faith to work hard. Of course, there is a balance of times when we work and times when we don't. When we do, may we use what we earn for those around us as well as ourselves.

May we be blessed in our giving and be even more generous than before. When we partner our faith with action, we show what we truly value and believe. May one of our guiding values be the generosity of giving to those in need. May we provide for those we can and practice offering excess to those who have less than we do. We partner with Christ when we do.

Jesus, I want to know the deep joy of partnering with your heart in practical ways. As I become more generous and intentional with what I have, may your joy rise within me.

CONTINUAL SURRENDER

"Whoever wants to be my disciple must deny themselves
and take up their cross and follow me."
MATTHEW 16:24 NIV

Following Jesus requires more than a one-time surrender.
We must continually submit our hearts and lives to him.
We are constantly learning, reassessing, and maturing. We
most likely know more now than we did a year ago. Why
would we assume our faith is static?

In an ever-changing world that pulls us in many directions,
may we yield our hearts to the Lord and let his values
underpin our choices no matter how far we have veered
off-course. God is not offended by our humanity. He is
more gracious with us than we are with ourselves. Give
yourself over to his kind, patient, and wise leadership.

Lord Jesus, I submit myself to your guidance today. I
don't want to hold so tightly to my rights that I miss out
on the power of your love. I choose to follow you no
matter what it costs me. You are worth it.

ALL THINGS POSSIBLE

"If you can believe,
all things are possible to him who believes."
MARK 9:23 NKJV

This is an amazing statement from Jesus. When we believe, all things are possible. The sky becomes the limit. We are well-practiced at diminishing our disappointment, but how much do we trust the power of God to work in our lives?

Isaiah 40:28-31 says, "Have you not known? Have you not heard? The everlasting God, the Lord, the Creator of the ends of the earth, neither faints nor is weary. His understanding is unsearchable. He gives power to the weak…those who wait on the Lord shall renew their strength." There are no limits to those who believe. Let your faith be encouraged by the faithfulness of God, for he can do what no one else can. He is mighty, majestic, and equally loving.

Christ Jesus, increase my faith as I follow you. You are immovable, unchangeable, and wonderful. I trust you more than I trust myself. Thank you for the miracles of mercy you do and will continue to do.

UNDISTRACTED

"You won't need to take anything with you—trust in God
alone. And don't get distracted from my purpose
by anyone you might meet along the way."
LUKE 10:4 TPT

When Jesus sends us, he gives us all we need for the
journey. Sometimes, he will give specific instructions
on what to take. Other times, he will tell us to trust his
provision and leave everything behind. Whatever we do or
don't bring along, Jesus' advice not to get distracted from
his purpose applies to us today.

What has God called you to do? How focused have you
remained on his purposes? Receive the grace that is yours,
be undistracted by competing interests, and focus on his
goals. In a world of distractions, it takes concentrated effort
and firm boundaries to remain steadfast to the important
things. Take it seriously with necessary, practical steps.

Lord, I need your help and grace today. Refresh my
vision and remind me what is most important. As you
do, help me refine my focus by putting up boundaries
and holding them. Thank you for your help.

FOR LOVE'S SAKE

"God did not send his Son into the world
to condemn the world, but in order that
the world might be saved through him."
JOHN 3:17 ESV

God the Father sent Jesus, his Son, into the world so we might know what he is like. He sent him not to condemn us but to save us. 1 John 4:9-10 explains it like this: "God sent his only Son into the world, so that we might live through him. In this is love, not that we have loved God but that he loved us and sent his Son to be the propitiation for our sins."

God loved us long before we loved him. He was compelled by pure compassion to send us his Son. In love, we get to respond to this beautiful, divinely generous invitation. Our new lives are empowered by the faith of Jesus Christ who loves us so much he gave himself for us and lives in us. Powerful and loving grace has saved us; we can't save ourselves.

Lord Jesus, thank you for the love you reveal to us. Open the eyes of my understanding so I may know how wide, deep, long, and high your loyal love is.

JUSTICE FOR THE OPPRESSED

"I tell you that He will bring about justice
for them quickly. However, when the Son of Man comes,
will He find faith on the earth?"

LUKE 18:8 NASB

Jesus loves justice. He does not side with tyrannical systems. He stands with the oppressed, and we must align our hearts and stances with his. We don't want to blindly follow people who claim to have our best interests at heart while also keeping the poor in their place.

Worldly politics don't reflect the government of our God. Jesus is King, and he reigns with justice, mercy, and truth. He does not manipulate or rule with fear. He is endlessly patient with us. He is better to us than we are to each other. We can't ignore his call to stand for justice, promote peace, and demand accountability from those who abuse their power. May we join with God's heart and work as the hands and feet of our Lord Jesus Christ.

Almighty King, your love is both truthful and powerful. You do not ignore the cries of the needy or oppressed; I know you will answer them. Show me how to partner with you in justice on this earth.

SERVANT LEADERSHIP

"Whoever wants to be a leader among you must be
your servant, and whoever wants to be first
among you must become your slave."
MATTHEW 20:26-27 NLT

Leadership advice that doesn't make serving others a
priority is not worth listening to. The greatest leader is
Jesus, and he spent his entire life serving others. If we
want to follow his example, we must be willing to do what
others don't want to do. There are no shortcuts to a life of
integrity; step by step, we have to do the work.

What drives us? If we don't have a passion for what we are
doing, along with a good work ethic and a team-oriented
mindset, we won't last. We can learn from the successes
and mistakes of others, but we must also do the work. We
can find our purpose rooted deep in our hearts where the
Spirit fuels us with his kingdom desires.

Jesus, I won't give in to the trap of thinking lasting
success happens by accident. I choose to partner with
you in servant-hearted leadership. Keep me on your
path, Jesus.

IN THE SAME WAY

"The Son of Man did not come to be served.
He came to serve others and to give his life
as a ransom for many people."
MATTHEW 20:28 NCV

If the King of kings didn't think himself above serving others, how can we think anything is beneath us? Compassion gets down in the dirt. It shows practical kindness to people often overlooked. It's more concerned with others than with personal comfort. Compassion compelled Christ to leave his throne and humble himself as a human. It led him to the cross.

In the same way Christ did not come to be served, may we reject the pull to satisfy ourselves at all costs. If we don't have a larger view, the perspective of Christ, we will fall into traps of self-satisfaction. As we serve others, Jesus meets us with the abundance of his Spirit. Everything we need can be found in him. We don't do this by our own strength either; he is our help.

Jesus, I look to your example for how to live. Fill me with your grace and help me.

BE ALERT

"You must watch!
I have told you everything in advance."
MARK 13:23 CSB

Jesus prophesied about many things that will happen in the last days. He said there will be suffering, false reports of the Messiah returning, and persecution of those who believe in him. We should not be surprised if such things happen, for he warned us they will. In fact, they are happening right now. No one knows when the last day will be.

What does it look like to be alert without giving in to fear? We can be on our guard, wise and discerning, and still be filled with the powerful love of God that keeps us steadfast. Being aware of greater forces at work grounds us in both the reality of Christ's kingdom and the reality of the earth's situation. May we not avoid harsh realities but instead be alert and stand our ground in peace and love.

Jesus, you are full of truth. You never lie. Even though I don't understand what all has to happen before you return again, I trust you are with me. Please ground my heart and mind in your wisdom and love.

CAREFUL LISTENING

"Consider carefully how you listen. Whoever has will be given more; whoever does not have, even what they think they have will be taken from them."

LUKE 8:18 NIV

In the kingdom of Christ, those who have will be given even more. Those who think they have everything will find, in the end, they have nothing. This isn't about material wealth; it's about spiritual wealth. We should be careful to listen to Christ with open hearts. Those who listen to truly understand will be given more revelation.

If we don't actively try to understand what God is saying, we may miss it altogether. It's like sitting with a friend and being consumed by our thoughts while they bare their hearts. In the end, we don't retain what they share with us, and the relationship is bruised. Let's keep our connection with Spirit open and listen to what he is sharing.

Lord, I don't want to miss out on what you are saying. Today, I position my heart before you as an open book for you to write in. Speak; I am listening.

BEFORE THEIR TIME

"Dear woman, why come to me?
My time has not yet come."
JOHN 2:4 NKJV

Jesus attended a wedding with his mother and disciples. This was before Jesus had done any major miracles. When the hosts ran out of wine because of all the guests in attendance, Mary asked Jesus to do something about it. In today's verse, we find Jesus' response. Everything would change for him if he unveiled his power.

Did Jesus refuse? No. Jesus honored his mother's request and turned water into wine. It was the first of many extraordinary miracles Jesus performed, and it revealed his glory. Don't be afraid to ask Jesus to intervene in a situation where your heart is moved. He turned water into wine to honor his mother's request, and he may move on your behalf too.

Jesus, I'm astounded by this story. I can't understand why you would do it, yet what an act of love it was. Give me revelation to understand you; give me courage to not only ask you for greater things but to trust you with them.

ANSWER TO PRAYER

Jesus said to the centurion, "Go;
it shall be done for you as you have believed."
And the servant was healed at that very moment.
MATTHEW 8:13 NASB

When Jesus encountered the Roman centurion, he found faith that surprised him. In fact, he said, "I have not found such great faith with anyone in Israel" (vs. 10). The Roman soldier knew what authority really meant; a person in charge could say, "do this," and it would be done. While Jesus offered to go with him, the centurion merely asked for him to give the authoritative word. In answer to his request, Jesus released healing with a word, and the moment he said it, the servant was healed.

The authority of Christ is as powerful today. We don't need to physically touch Jesus to receive the power of his Word. He releases it, and we experience its effects. Isaiah 55:11 supports this: "My word which goes out of My mouth; It will not return to Me empty, without accomplishing what I desire, and without succeeding in the purpose for which I sent it."

Powerful One, what mighty authority you have! With just a word, you can change everything and set in motion circumstances to serve your kingdom.

ALL IS FORGIVEN

"Truly I say to you, all sins will be forgiven the sons and daughters of men, and whatever blasphemies they commit."
MARK 3:28 NASB

The mercy of Christ covers our sins. Yes, every single one. He forgives what we struggle to forgive in ourselves. In him, we find the light of life, freedom from sin, and the incredible power to offer the same generous mercy to others.

Jesus said in Luke 7:47 that those who have been forgiven for many sins know how to love well. Those who assume they have little to be forgiven will love little. Love is shown in how we express it to others and not just in how we receive it. When we have been shown great mercy, are we not more ready to offer it to others? Far be it for us to withhold from others what has been freely lavished on us.

Merciful Jesus, may I never withhold forgiveness from others and especially from those who ask it of me. I want to be merciful like you. Align my life with your living truth.

RECEIVE CARE

"Remain in the same house, eating and drinking what
they provide, for the laborer deserves his wages.
Do not go from house to house."
LUKE 10:7 ESV

When Jesus sent out his seventy followers to minister to
the surrounding towns and prepare the way for his arrival,
he gave specific instructions. One of the instructions was
how to receive the hospitality of people whose homes
they stayed in. It is right for us to freely receive the care
others show for us.

Hospitality is a wonderful way to both display and receive
the kindness of Christ. Whether we are on the giving
or receiving end, may we recognize the importance of
generously sharing with others. It is a beautiful reflection
of what it means to be in God's family.

Lord Jesus, I don't want resist in my heart when
others show me hospitality. I don't want to hold back
hospitality either. Make me willing to receive and give
service to reflect your kindness and goodness.

PROPER SIGHT

"I entered this world to render judgment—
to give sight to the blind and to show those
who think they see that they are blind."
JOHN 9:39 NLT

Jesus came to put wrong perspectives right. Those who thought they saw clearly, Jesus made blind. If they were to acknowledge their blindness at any time, their sin would be removed (vs. 41). For those who had no clear picture of God, Jesus came to give them sight. He opened their eyes to see and believe who the Father truly is.

Pride kept these blinded people stuck in their sin. If only they would humble themselves before Jesus, he would remove their sin and give them true understanding. Does pride keep us from knowing God in spirit and truth? May we humble our hearts before him today and receive the freedom his mercy brings.

Lord Jesus, I want to know you, worship you, and walk with you in spirit and truth. I humble my heart before you. I don't know better than you; I need your help. Open my eyes to understand your character and kingdom.

HOME IN HEAVEN

"The foxes have holes to live in, and the birds have nests, but the Son of Man has no place to rest his head."
MATTHEW 8:20 NCV

During his ministry years, Jesus wandered from place to place. He didn't have a home to go back to at the end of the day. His home, he knew, was in heaven with his Father. He would continue the assignment he had been given until the day he returned home.

Hebrews 13:14 says, "Here on earth we do not have a city that lasts forever, but we are looking for the city that we will have in the future." Our true home awaits us in the coming of Jesus' kingdom to earth. In eternity, we will dwell with him and have no more pain, sickness, or grief. We will know him as clearly as we are known by God. When life's storms rock us to the core, we can look ahead to the eternal realm awaiting us. We will dwell in the house of our God forever, and it will be glorious.

Jesus, you are my true home. While I journey through this temporary time on earth, keep my eyes fixed on you as the originator and finisher of my faith. You are my vision, and my hope is in you.

NO RIGHT

When they persisted in questioning him, he stood up and
said to them, "The one without sin among you should be
the first to throw a stone at her."

JOHN 8:7 CSB

One day while Jesus was teaching, the Pharisees dragged
an adulterous woman into the middle of the crowd. They
explained how they had found her, and they recited
Moses' law that required the woman be stoned to death.
They asked Jesus what they should do with her. This was a
test, and they wanted to trap him.

Jesus' next move was to write in the dust with his finger.
We don't know what he wrote, but we do know what he
said next. "Let anyone among you without sin be the first
to throw a stone at her." Jesus was rewriting the script
the Pharisees so zealously acted out. In the end, not one
accuser remained, and no one threw a stone. If they had
no right to condemn another, even though she had been
caught in her sin, what right do we have?

Jesus, how I wish I could know what you wrote in the
dust! Even so, the point is clear. I humble my heart
before you, and I refuse to ignore the log in my own eye
while pointing out the splinter in another's eye.

HUMBLE YOURSELF

"I tell you that this man, rather than the other, went home justified before God. For all those who exalt themselves will be humbled, and those who humble themselves will be exalted."

LUKE 18:14 NIV

God does not care about our loud displays of worship or service; he cares about the state of our hearts. Jesus described two very different men offering God their prayers. One, a religious one, thanked God that he wasn't like others. He was basically bragging in his prayer. The other, a tax collector, stood at a distance, beat his breast, and asked God to have mercy on him.

The tax collector was justified before God not because he said the right words but because his heart was pure and humble. God can't be distracted from what we actually value. Let's humble ourselves before him, as the tax collector did, and find justification through Christ.

Jesus, I won't put on a show for you today. I simply come as I am with a humble heart to seek forgiveness and freedom. Have mercy on me, a sinner.

SOUGHT AND SAVED

"The Son of Man has come
to save that which was lost."
MATTHEW 18:11 NKJV

Jesus came to look for the lost. He came to save those who feel alone in this world. Psalm 68:6 says, "God sets the solitary in families; He brings out those who are bound into prosperity." He puts the lonely in families and leads prisoners into prosperous joy. That's the hope we have in Jesus.

However alone you feel today, Jesus sees you, and he comes to your rescue. Lean on him. He is closer than you realize. He offers you the peace of his presence and the joy of his fellowship. He sees where you are, and he comes to you. Look up and find his steady hand of love reaching out to you today.

Savior, thank you for caring about the lost and lonely of this world and coming to save us. I am undone by your goodness. Meet me with the power of your presence and love me to life once more.

NO CONDEMNATION

*"I do not condemn you, either. Go.
From now on do not sin any longer."*
JOHN 8:11 NASB

There is no condemnation in Christ. This was true when Jesus walked among the people, and it is true now that he is seated at the right hand of his Father in heaven. What Jesus does not condemn in us, let us not condemn either. In the love of Christ, there is freedom.

Our freedom leads us to live for Christ. His ways are best, and his values are eternal. As 1 Peter 2:16 says, "Act as free people, and do not use your freedom as a covering for evil, but use it as bond-servants of God." We choose how we will live. Let's choose what is best for Christ, his kingdom, and for us.

Christ, thank you for the freedom I have in your love. Thank you for not condemning me in my sin. You are my liberator, and I will spend my time living for your kingdom.

DEEPER UNDERSTANDING

"You do not know what you are asking.
Are you able to drink the cup that I am to drink?"
MATTHEW 20:22 ESV

Sometimes when we ask the Lord for something, we don't know the extent of what we are truly asking. In these moments, we may hear the Lord say, as he said to James, John, and their mother: "You do not know what you are asking." What seems a simple ask to us may have a significant cost. Are we willing to pay up?

The only way to walk in the fullness of faith is to submit ourselves to Christ and his leadership no matter what it costs us. We must take him seriously, for he knows better than we do. Following Christ is fulfilling, but it's not easy when the world urges us toward ambivalence and apathy. Take up your cross and follow him, for in him is the fullness of life.

Jesus, thank you for being honest and kind even when I have no idea what I am asking of you. Thank you for your goodness. I don't want to follow anyone else. With you is life, peace, joy, and hope.

TRUE CHILD OF GOD

"Life has come to you and your household, for you are a true son of Abraham. The Son of Man has come to seek out and to give life to those who are lost."

LUKE 19:9-10 TPT

When Jesus entered Zacchaeus' home, he was welcomed joyously. Zacchaeus was amazed that Jesus would visit him. He was so overwhelmed by this gracious act, he told Jesus, "Half of all that I own I will give to the poor. And Lord, if I have cheated anyone, I promise to pay back four times as much as I stole" (vs. 8).

This confessional promise is a picture of the salvation life that had come to Zacchaeus and his household. A man who was known as a crook turned from his wicked ways and promised to pay generous restitution. This was an act of beautiful surrender to the lordship of Jesus, and Jesus didn't even ask him for it. His active repentance was an indication of the readiness of his heart.

Jesus, I will not withhold anything from you. I am met by your gracious presence, and I vow to change in major ways to honor you and those who I have wronged.

BELIEF STARTS SOMEWHERE

"If you don't believe me when I tell you about
earthly things, how can you possibly believe
if I tell you about heavenly things?"

JOHN 3:12 NLT

Jesus brings practical wisdom. His kingdom is represented
in this world if we have eyes to see it. The mercy of God
weaves through the fabric of our lives, and we are woven
together in the great tapestry of his love. He includes what
seems insignificant to us. He spares no detail.

If you are having trouble believing God about things that
feel too far-off to understand, ask for understanding about
how he meets you here and now. Faith grows, but that
growth has to start somewhere. Nurture the seed planted
in your heart. Every step matters.

Jesus, thank you for meeting me where I am and leading
me forward. Though I feel lost when I consider where I
am and where I want to go, you are there at every step.
Open my eyes to your presence even in the messiest
areas of my life.

TAKE COURAGE

"Don't be afraid. Go and tell my followers to go on to
Galilee, and they will see me there."
MATTHEW 28:10 NCV

When Jesus encountered the women on their way to relay
the news of his resurrection to his disciples, they were
overwhelmed with adoration. They bowed before him and
grasped his feet. They were filled with deep wonder and
joy at just the mention of his resurrection; imagine how
that grew when he appeared!

When Jesus meets us, whether in our sorrow or joy, his
presence brings peace. He tells us to throw off all our fears.
The hope of his resurrection life lives on today. We can lay
aside every fear and walk in the confidence of his Word.
When he gives us an assignment, he gives us his presence
and strength to complete it.

Jesus, what wonder and deep relief those women must
have felt at seeing you alive and well. Every hope they
had was riding on you, and you did not disappoint. I
know you won't disappoint me either. I love you, Lord.

NOVEMBER

"The thief's purpose
is to steal and kill and destroy.
My purpose is to give them
a rich and satisfying life."

JOHN 10:10 NLT

WORDS AND DEEDS

"Evil originates from inside a person.
Coming out of a human heart are evil schemes,
sexual immorality, theft, murder, adultery, greed,
wickedness, treachery, debauchery, jealousy,
slander, arrogance, and recklessness."

MARK 7:21-22 TPT

If you think you are a good person, look at how you speak about and to others. If you believe you are faultless, look at your daily actions and the intentions behind them. This is not meant to shame you but to ground you. What makes you holy isn't what you do; it's what comes out of your heart.

As we submit our hearts to Christ, he transforms us in his living love. Our words and deeds are reflections of the state of our hearts, so we shouldn't ignore them. When we notice we are being harsher with people, it's a hint that we need to tend to our hearts. When we freely slander others, it is a sign that our hearts are out of alignment with Christ's mercy. Today, let's offer him our hearts and adjust our attitudes.

Jesus, wash over my heart in the power of your love. I want to reflect you and live in the freedom of your merciful kindness.

BREAKING BREAD

"I have eagerly desired to eat this Passover
with you before I suffer."
LUKE 22:15 NIV

Jesus had been looking forward to the Passover meal with
his disciples. It would be a significant time with his dear
friends. He would teach them the power of breaking bread
together. He would make a new covenant using his body
and blood.

How often do we feast with those we love? Are we too
busy to take time for people important to us? Make it a
priority to gather, especially at important times of feasting,
to share food, company, faith, and love with one another.
It's a privilege to belong to others and them to us.

Lord, I love that you were excited to celebrate Passover
with your disciples. You knew you would suffer; this would
be a precious time of fellowship, covenants, and feasting.
Every time I have the privilege of breaking bread with
those I love, I will think of you and honor you in it.

NOTHING TO PROVE

"I spoke openly to the world. I always taught in synagogues and in the temple, where the Jews always meet, and in secret I have said nothing."

JOHN 18:20 NKJV

When Jesus was brought before the high priest, he asked what Jesus had been teaching his followers. In response, Jesus said he had spoken in public for all to hear. He did not defend himself with details. He had nothing to prove.

When we live with integrity, we have nothing to hide. The traps others lay for us are feeble ones at best. We can't stop a vendetta against us, but we can trust God to defend our character. We need not give lengthy receipts of things already in the open for all to see. May we trust God with our lives even when some try to destroy our character. Standing on the firm foundation of truth and love, we have nothing to hide, and we need not live in fear.

Jesus, I want to be full of integrity, so no threat of exposure has any merit. Thank you for the strength of your mercy that fuels my life and my trust.

ABOVE REPROACH

"So that we do not offend them, go to the sea and throw in a hook, and take the first fish that comes up; and when you open its mouth, you will find a stater. Take that and give it to them for you and Me."

MATTHEW 17:27 NASB

Jesus did not live above the law even though he rightfully could. Why would then we look for ways to sidestep our responsibilities as citizens of earthly nations? Jesus paid the taxes required of him, and we should as well.

When we live above reproach, doing the right thing as often as we can, we show that the power of God's truth has made its way into our hearts. Excuses made to avoid our responsibilities reflect self-interest. Instead, may we humbly live, correct ourselves when we stray, and rely on God's grace to transform us.

Jesus, I am amazed at how practical you are. What I do with my money matters to you, and I don't want to avoid my responsibility to the government out of a sense of scarcity. Give me a right mindset; help me to choose the right thing.

PATIENT TEACHER

"Was it not necessary that the Christ should suffer these things and enter into his glory?"
LUKE 24:26 ESV

The Scriptures foretold that the Messiah would suffer. There was no getting around the prophetic declarations in Scripture saying it would happen. However, Jesus' victorious resurrection was also prophesied.

The Scriptures pointed to what Christ would go through. Even after his resurrection, Jesus taught two of his disciples what the Scriptures had said while their minds were still clouded with grief. They did not recognize him until he broke bread with them, and they were astonished. Jesus, the ever-patient teacher, sits with us and corrects us as we listen to him. Keep your heart open to him.

Great Teacher, I don't want to stop learning from you. There is more I do not know than I do know. It's laughable how little I know. Teach me your ways, Jesus. Teach me the truth.

GOD'S FAMILY

Looking in the eyes of those who were sitting in a circle around him, he said, "Here are my true family members. For whoever does the will of God is my brother, my sister, and my mother!"

MARK 3:34-35 TPT

No matter how close we are to our earthly families, some of us will never fit into the molds our families make for us. Jesus, full of love for his family, also made it clear that his chosen family were the ones who followed God. Those who hungered and thirsted for righteousness were his people.

Perhaps you have friends who share the same values as you. Don't they feel closer than flesh and blood in some ways? When we have a shared vision, the bond goes deep. Even if you struggle to find your place in groups, remember you are part of God's family if you have submitted your life to Christ. In him, you have a true home.

Jesus, thank you for making connections between people with a shared heart and vision. Family isn't always easy to deal with, but it is where we grow. May I find maturity, belonging, and my place in your family.

LIKE OLD TIMES

He called out, "Fellows,
have you caught any fish?"
JOHN 21:5 NLT

This is a simple greeting; it's familiar and casual. It's Jesus in good humor reaching out to old friends who have not recognized him yet. When the disciples were in their grief, they didn't know what to do with themselves. So, they went back to a familiar pastime: fishing.

The setting: dawn at the Sea of Galilee. The disciples were on the boat, and Jesus called out to them from shore, "Fellows, have you caught any fish?" When they replied no, he told them to throw their net on the right side of the boat. When they realized who it was, they went to shore (hauling more fish than they could carry). Then, they had breakfast together. Just Jesus and his friends like old times. When we don't know what to do, we might hear Jesus calling out to us as old friends do.

Loving Jesus, meet me with your persistent presence. Speak to me as you did at first, and I will come running. I need your refreshing perspective to transform mine.

MERCY MEETS US

"People who believe in God's Son are not judged guilty. Those who do not believe have already been judged guilty, because they have not believed in God's one and only Son."

JOHN 3:18 NCV

In the light of God's love revealed in Christ, we have a choice. Will we believe in the Son of God, Jesus Christ, or will we love our ways more than him? Jesus offers abundant life, generous grace, and the power of his forgiveness. What do we gain when we resist him?

Jesus said in John 12:25, "Those who love their life in this world will lose it. Those who care nothing for their life in this world will keep it for eternity" (NLT). Will we let go of the need to control every inch of our lives—which we most certainly can't do anyhow—and let the power of Christ transform us from the inside out? Mercy meets us now, and God's generous grace is near to empower us in following the ways of his kingdom.

King Jesus, there is no one else like you. You are the Son of God, and I submit my life to your leading. I trust you more than I trust my own ability to control anything.

SPECIFIC GRACE

"Not everyone is meant to remain single—only those whom God gives grace to be unmarried. For some are born to celibacy; others have been made eunuchs by others. And there are some who have chosen to live in celibacy for the sacred purpose of heaven's kingdom realm. Let those who can, accept this truth for themselves."

MATTHEW 19:11-12 TPT

Not all of us are meant to be married; not all of us will remain single for life. There is specific grace for each of us. We will not miss out on what is for us, and there is strength for each season we experience.

If you find yourself in a situation you feel ill-equipped to handle, know that God is with you. He has grace for your specific circumstances. Don't rely on your limits when God is ready to flood you with his love. Your worth does not change when your relationship status does. You are always worthy of love, and the great fountain of God's passionate love flows over you today.

Jesus, thank you for the grace you give through your Spirit. Give me your perspective over my circumstances and my longings and help me rest in trust and gratitude for what is already mine.

LIGHT OF LIFE

"I am the light of the world.
Whoever follows me will never walk in darkness,
but will have the light of life."
JOHN 8:12 NIV

When we follow Jesus, we do not walk in the darkness of this world or its ways. We have the light of his life lighting our steps. As Psalm 119:105 puts it, "Your word is a lamp for my feet, a light on my path." Jesus is the living Word, and he shows us the way to go.

If there is a decision you have been struggling to make, look to the Lord today. Ask for his insight. Sometimes in the light of God's presence, we will see multiple options to move forward. Other times, we will only see one possible way. Do we trust his leadership? We need not fear making a wrong choice, for if we keep relying on his leadership, he will maneuver us around and through obstacles and help us when a new start comes. He is the light of life for every person who believes.

Light of Life, thank you for illuminating the path before me. Give me peace and confidence as I follow you into what feels like the great unknown.

DEEP ROOTS

"These likewise are the ones sown on stony ground who, when they hear the word, immediately receive it with gladness; and they have no root in themselves, and so endure only for a time. Afterward, when tribulation or persecution arises for the word's sake, immediately they stumble."

MARK 4:16-17 NKJV

When we receive the gospel of Christ with gladness, it's a good start. However, if we are not rooted in the love of Christ through our experience, we will not endure the test of time. What does it take to persevere under pressure?

Psalm 1 may give us some clues. It talks about not walking in ungodly counsel but delighting in the law of the Lord. It says those who meditate on it day and night will be blessed like a tree planted by a river. If we want our roots to grow deep, we must nourish our hearts with the words of Christ. We must know God for ourselves. In this relationship, we will not only be able to stand the test of time, but we will flourish.

Jesus, teach me your ways, and reveal your truth to me as I meditate on your Word. I want to grow deep roots in your love.

HIGHER KINGDOM

"My kingdom is not of this world. If My kingdom were
of this world, My servants would be fighting so that
I would not be handed over to the Jews; but as it is,
My kingdom is not of this realm."

JOHN 18:36 NASB

The kingdom of Christ is not based in the systems of this
world. It is not like earthly governments or palaces. It is far
better; it fights spiritual darkness and evil. Citizens of Christ's
kingdom do not fight as the world fights. Paul said in
Ephesians 6:12, "our struggle is not against flesh and blood."

Do we truly live like this, or do we fight with the best of
them? May we remain rooted in the kingdom of Christ
and his power to overcome every battle that comes our
way. With the strategy and wisdom of Christ, we can rise
above fights that consume others. We don't need to make
enemies out of neighbors when Christ has called us to
love others as we love ourselves.

Heavenly King, prayer is my battle ground where I
lay out all my questions and struggles. Help me resist
making enemies of those I'm meant to work with.
Thank you for your higher perspective. If I get lost
in the weeds, broaden my view.

WHERE YOU BELONG

"Why were you looking for me?
Did you not know that I must be in my Father's house?"
LUKE 2:49 ESV

Jesus was perfectly without sin, but he was not the perfect child according to human standards. Would such a child disregard his parents' concerns and choose to stay in a large city on his own? When Mary and Joseph realized Jesus had not left Jerusalem with them, they retraced their steps and anxiously searched for their twelve-year-old.

Can we fault Jesus for wanting to be in the house of his Father? He must have connected deeply with God in that place. When we are compelled by a deep longing to stay when others would have us rush on, is it not right to honor the truth within us? When we learn to trust the Spirit, we can confidently make choices that reflect his guidance.

Jesus, when I feel a deep longing rise within me to either stay in a place or go to a specific one, help me trust the wisdom behind it. I want to honor your truth with the depths of my being even when others don't understand.

ALL AUTHORITY

Jesus came close to them and said,
"All the authority of the universe has been given to me."
MATTHEW 28:18 TPT

After Jesus rose from the grave, defeating sin and death, the resurrection power of his fulfillment meant he was finished with his assignment on earth. He was given all the authority of the universe, and he holds it still. Jesus has the power to commission us in his name. He has the authority to do more than we can imagine.

May we not hesitate in his presence but embrace him as the loving Lord he is. When we walk in his ways, teaching others to do the same, we honor the legacy of his ministry and the power of his life in us. No power can overcome him, and he has authority over everyone. As David said in Psalm 27, "The Lord is my light and my salvation—whom shall I fear?"

Powerful One, as I walk in the light of your salvation, there is nothing to fear. Keep me close to your heart and walking in your ways. I trust you.

WHAT YOU LOVE

"The judgment is based on this fact: God's light came into the world, but people loved the darkness more than the light, for their actions were evil."

JOHN 3:19 NLT

When we love something, we will show it with how we live. Do we love God's light more than we do the darkness? The light of God's love is powerful, pure, and freeing. It's full of good fruit: peace, joy, patience, kindness, gentleness, and self-control. There is more satisfaction in his marvelous mercy than in anything we could gain on our own.

We focus our attention on what we love, so look at your life. What does it say about where your affections lie? It's not too late to change. It's not too difficult to fine-tune. Submit to the light of Christ. He is good. He is worth it.

Jesus, show me the power of your love today in ways I've never known. Reveal yourself to me and open my heart to your revealing light. I want my love for you to be evident in my life.

IMPOSSIBLE MERCY

"Father, forgive them,
because they don't know what they are doing."
LUKE 23:34 NCV

As Jesus was dying on the cross, he prayed for his tormenters. He prayed the Father would forgive them because they didn't realize what they were doing. It was an impossible display of mercy. There is understanding in the heart of God for the ways we fall short. Even unto death, Christ's mercy was unstoppable.

May we follow in his footsteps with those who hurt us. We can forgive them as Christ forgave us. Even when it's difficult to understand why others do what they do, pray for God's mercy to intervene in their lives. There is an unending supply of forgiveness in the heart of God.

Merciful Jesus, I can't imagine looking at the people who were actively murdering me and praying for the Father to forgive them. I want to be so enveloped in your love that I choose to pray for those who harm me. Help me, Jesus. Immerse me in your impossible mercy.

READY FOR A VISIT

"Go into the city to a certain man," he said, "and tell him,
'The Teacher says: My time is near; I am celebrating the
Passover at your place with my disciples.'"
MATTHEW 26:18 CSB

Jesus wants us to fellowship freely with him. Is there a
place for him in our hearts and lives? No matter how
crowded our lives, we have to make room. Christ has
already made the provisions and prepared a way to feast
with him.

Are we ready for the Spirit of God to redirect us today? We
must always be ready to do what the Spirit says and follow
through in humble obedience. God does everything with
purpose, love, and power. Even as we make room in our
lives and remain ready, God is doing everything to provide
us with all we need.

Jesus, I make room in my heart for your presence. With
your help, I can make myself ready to follow your voice.
The more I know you, the more I love you; the more I
love you, the more eager I am to do your will.

FLESH AND BONES

"Look at my hands and my feet. It is I myself!
Touch me and see; a ghost does not have
flesh and bones, as you see I have."
LUKE 24:39 NIV

Even in Jesus' resurrected body, he has flesh and bones.
This gives us a glimpse into how we will transform in his
glory as we enter eternity. We don't suddenly lose the
makeup of what makes us human. As 1 Corinthians 15
says, we are transformed into our new bodies and raised
in glory.

Knowing our bodies are the seeds of what we will receive,
let's learn to honor our earthly bodies. When we hate our
bodies, we don't reflect the kingdom of Christ. We can love
and honor ourselves as much as Jesus loves and honors
us. Our bodies are amazing! They are made in the image
of God and intricately woven together. There is more at
work within our cells than we are aware of. Our bodies are
beautiful to behold.

Jesus, I want to honor this body of mine and cultivate
love and gratitude for it. Please heal my relationship
with my body. I know it reflects the body to come.

COME AND EAT

Jesus said to them, "Come and eat breakfast." Yet none of
the disciples dared ask Him, "Who are You?"—
knowing that it was the Lord.
JOHN 21:12 NKJV

Jesus invited the disciples to sit and eat with him. We
overlook the simple and natural sometimes, don't we? This
gesture is surprisingly touching. Sharing a meal together
is incredibly connective. It's a spiritual act as much as a
natural one.

When was the last time you invited friends over for a
meal? It can be a simple time to bond with others. We
can't avoid eating; we need sustenance. If we use these
times to connect with each other rather than rush through
them to get back to work or our to-do lists, we may come
away refreshed and full in more ways than one.

Jesus, I recognize how relational you were, and I don't
want to miss out on the deeper connections I can have
in my own life with a little more intentionality. Help me
prioritize relationships and follow through on quality
time with others.

NEW UNDERSTANDING

"The next time we drink this, I will be with you and we
will drink it together with a new understanding in the
kingdom realm of my Father."
MATTHEW 26:29 TPT

Jesus taught his disciples to take communion together.
Communion is a powerful act of remembrance that honors
the sacrifice Jesus gave for the freedom of those who come
to the Father through him. We eat the bread and drink
from the cup, and we honor Christ who died for us.

Not only do we honor his sacrifice in communion, but we
also look forward to the power of his resurrection in our
lives. Jesus promised his disciples would drink together
with him in the kingdom realm of his Father. This is our
promise too. There, we will have deeper understanding of
Christ's incredible love for us. Until then, let's not neglect
the practice of communion together.

Savior, thank you for the beautiful practice of communion;
it centers our attention on your sacrifice and the power
of it. Thank you for the hope of resurrection. I honor you,
worship you, and submit to you.

I WILL SHOW YOU

"Follow Me, and I will have you
become fishers of people."
MARK 1:17 NASB

Jesus shows us how to use his skills for his kingdom. He is the greatest teacher. He doesn't tell us to change what we do and then walk away while we attempt it. He beckons us to follow him, and he invites us to learn from him. He spends time teaching us the ways of his kingdom. In this divine relationship, transformation happens.

When we are trying to make a change, it is important we learn from those who know how to do it. We don't have to rely on ourselves when we can learn in the context of connection and relationship. Let's humble our hearts and learn from those who have more wisdom, skills, and knowledge than we do.

Jesus, show me how to live for you. I want to walk confidently, knowing who you called me to be, while relying on your leadership to help me mature.

HIS GLORIOUS HOME

"Even if I do bear witness about myself, my testimony is true, for I know where I came from and where I am going, but you do not know where I come from or where I am going."
JOHN 8:14 ESV

Jesus knew where he came from and where he was going. He knew where his true home was, and no one could convince him otherwise. Jesus didn't need the approval or agreement of humans to prove to him what he already knew to be true.

Do we have the same kind of conviction about where we belong? When we live according to our values, some will misunderstand us; some will flat out hate us for it. It's not our job to convince others of the truth but to live it out with grounded confidence. We need not shape-shift to appease others. That's like trying to hit a constantly moving target. Jesus didn't feel the need to adjust himself to others' expectations. He lived truly with conviction and overflowing grace.

Jesus, I don't want to change who I am to suit others. May I live with conviction in the truth alive within me: who you have called me to be and who you are.

SPIRITUAL HUNGER

"What wealth is offered to you when you feel your spiritual poverty! For there is no charge to enter the realm of heaven's kingdom."

MATTHEW 5:3 TPT

When we completely rely on God for all we need, we are poor in spirit. That's a good thing! It's good to recognize our lack and God's abundance to meet it. Spiritual hunger leads us to the King of kings. He has set a table and reserved a place for each of us. There is no reason to delay; the feast is waiting.

It is beautiful to trust God completely for what we need. It is powerful to fully surrender to him. He is our loving Father and King, and he can fill every longing we have. As we fill up on his presence and the fruit of his kingdom, we have more than enough to take back to our lives and share with others.

Mighty Provider, you have all I need. I won't wander and search for fullness in alleys when you have already prepared a feast where I am welcome. I know how much I need what you offer.

NO PAIN LASTS FOREVER

"Unless the Lord shortens that time of calamity, not a single person will survive. But for the sake of his chosen ones he has shortened those days."

MARK 13:20 NLT

Some experiences in life are so painful, we can't focus on anything else. When this happens, it's not often because we did something wrong. There is more happening in the world than we can control. The pain of humanity is not caused by any individual but rather a collection of factors.

Instead of looking for ways to escape, could we trust the Lord to meet us in our hurt? He can bring peace to our souls. Even when storms rage, he can breathe calm into our inner worlds. He brings comfort and relief, and we can trust him to never let us waste away. He is our strength and our help, and he promises that this too will pass.

Jesus, when the pain and troubles of the world are too heavy to bear, bring relief in the fresh, living water of your presence. Strengthen me from the inside out so I can stand strong in your love when disaster sweeps through. One day, there will be no more suffering, and I look forward to that day.

ULTIMATE OFFERING

Jesus cried out in a loud voice,
"Father, I give you my life."
After Jesus said this, he died.
LUKE 23:46 NCV

When Jesus had done everything, he gave God his life. In the end, he offered his last breath and surrendered his spirit to his Father. Everything Jesus had done was an offering to the Father. Everything Jesus accomplished, he did out of love for us. As God himself, his love came straight from the Father's heart.

There is no greater offering, either before or since, than Jesus laying down his life. Both his humanity and divinity were placed down as he did. Though a person may die for a cause they believe in, how many have resurrected from the grave afterward? Jesus came from God and returned to him to provide a way for us to come along.

Jesus Christ, thank you for the sacrifice of your blood and body. I can't thank you enough. Your resurrection life is the hope of my own. I offer you my life, Lord. You are worthy of every bit of it.

PURE VISION

"Blessed are the pure in heart,
for they will see God."
Matthew 5:8 csb

When our hearts and intentions are pure, we will find what we are looking for. We will see God. If we are clouded by competing interests, today is the perfect opportunity to ground ourselves in what is truly important. What areas of our lives do we want to sow? What do we want to be known for we are gone?

May we align our hearts, minds, and lives in the limitless love of Christ. As we do, the revelations of God are continually revealed as we seek him. How can we align? Jesus is our righteousness. Through him, our hearts become pure, and we can see God. As David prayed, so can we: "Create in me a clean heart, O God, and put a new and right spirit within me" (Psalm 51:10).

Lord God, purify my heart. Make me clean before you and reveal yourself to me. I want to walk in your ways all the days of my life, for knowing you is the purpose of it all.

PUT DOWN YOUR WEAPON

Jesus commanded Peter, "Put your sword away!
Shall I not drink the cup the Father has given me?"
JOHN 18:11 NIV

Jesus does not command us to take up arms for him. In fact, he tells us to be peacemakers. While this may surprise some of us, it is straight from the mouth of God. "Blessed are the peacemakers, for they will be called children of God" (Matthew 5:9). Later in the same chapter, Jesus went on to say, "do not resist an evil person. If anyone slaps you on the right cheek, turn to them the other cheek also" (vs. 39).

This is radical. Not only are we not to seek vengeance, but we are told to love our enemies. We must lay down the weapons we are wielding against others in the name of Jesus and listen to what he actually says. This includes any act that seeks to destroy someone else including the weapons of words. Are we willing to actually do what Jesus said we should?

Lord, your kingdom ways are revolutionary. You bring life, not death, through your mercy. May I choose to do the same. Help me, God.

PURSUE PEACE

"Blessed are the peacemakers,
For they shall be called sons of God."
MATTHEW 5:9 NKJV

It is no small thing to pursue peace. It is not weak to promote the ways of God. This is especially true of ways that directly oppose what society and culture teach. It takes strength to lay down what we feel are our rights to stand up to those we disagree with. The ways of Christ require humility, compassion, and kindness.

We don't get to pick and choose which of Christ's ways are true based on what we like. That's not what truth looks like. We must be willing to change our minds when God presents us with his greater truth. If we want to represent him well, as his children, we must submit to his correction. As we do, we learn what it looks like to truly promote and pursue peace on earth as it is in heaven.

Jesus, your peace does not avoid conflict; it simply refuses to react in the same manner. Teach me how to be a peacemaker for your kingdom.

KNOW THE WORD

"Have you never read what David did when he was in
need and he and his companions became hungry."
MARK 2:25 NASB

The Pharisees were quick to throw the laws of the Torah at
Jesus when they found him going against them. We know
Jesus was spotless, so we know he did not sin by appearing
to break rules set centuries earlier. Jesus was quick to set
the record straight. How? He acted as he did in the desert
when he was being tempted; he used the Word of God.

Looking at the Scriptures as if they are black and white is a
narrow way to do it. Jesus reminded the Pharisees to look
at the example of David when he ate sacred food from the
temple. Out of need, he broke the law, but God did not
punish him because it was necessary provision for him.
When you read Scripture, don't stop with familiar verses
and stories. Find the thread holding them all together.

Jesus, you are the living Word. What you say goes. May I
never hold my understanding in higher esteem than your
heart. Reveal the beauty of the breadth of your Word, and
may I never settle for soothing my own biases with it.

THE RIGHT THING

"Blessed are those who are persecuted for righteousness' sake, for theirs is the kingdom of heaven."
MATTHEW 5:10 ESV

It's always worth doing the right thing even when it means upsetting others. It's better to act in line with the values of Christ than to pacify people. We could face pushback or be slandered for doing so, but this does not mean we chose wrong.

1 Peter 3:17 echoes Jesus' sentiment: "It is better to suffer for doing good, if that should be God's will, than for doing evil." When our conscience is clear, we have no reason to be ashamed. However, those who persecute us do. We can rest assured that God sees every sacrifice and move we make in submission to his mercy. He will reward us even if we suffer a little while for it now.

Righteous One, embolden my heart and clear my conscience as I live with integrity. I want to choose the right thing; please teach me your ways. I submit to your leadership in every area of my life.

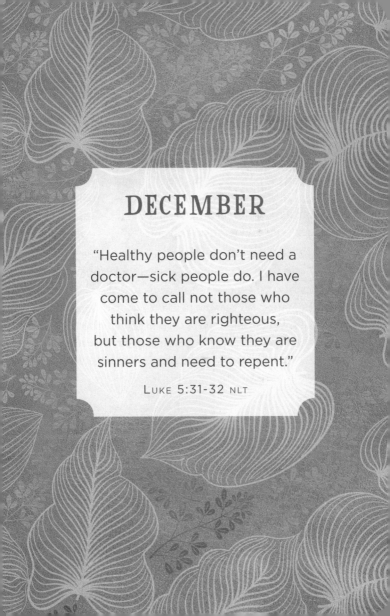

DECEMBER

"Healthy people don't need a
doctor—sick people do. I have
come to call not those who
think they are righteous,
but those who know they are
sinners and need to repent."

LUKE 5:31-32 NLT

THE REASON

"We have to go on to the surrounding villages so that I can give my message to the people there, for that is my mission."
MARK 1:38 TPT

Jesus knew the purpose of his life. He made choices about staying or moving according to it. What about us? Do we know the reason underlining our life? What factors help us make decisions about moving ahead?

There are seasons in life, and it's important to recognize we may make different choices in different seasons. That's okay! This was true for Jesus too. Jesus had a vision of what the Father had called him to do, and in this instance, he knew it was better to move on and spread his message rather than stay in a place where people wanted more of him. May we be willing to leave what is comfortable to accomplish the vision of our lives. Like Jesus' life, it takes focus and follow-through.

Jesus, give me a clear vision for this season of my life so I can make better choices and know when to move on. Thank you for your help.

GOOD FATHER

"If you sinful people know how to give good gifts to your children, how much more will your heavenly Father give good gifts to those who ask him."

MATTHEW 7:11 NLT

God gives the best gifts. He is a good, perfect father and not just an okay one. He has a never-ending abundance of resources to constantly draw from. His very being is love, so everything he gives is a representation of that.

If it doesn't look like love (and even kind correction does), then it probably isn't from God. How many things do we attribute to the Father that don't reflect his character? Sometimes we let thoughts of vengeance, exclusion, or manipulation into our understanding of God. God is not like that at all. Jesus revealed the heart of the Father, and it is just, patient, faithful, and merciful.

Christ Jesus, thank you for setting the record straight when it comes to what God is like. You are what God is like, and you are wonderful. Transform my understanding in the grace of your presence. I want to know you more.

KNOWING GOD

They asked, "Where is your father?" Jesus answered,
"You don't know me or my Father. If you knew me,
you would know my Father, too."
JOHN 8:19 NCV

To understand what God is like, we need look no further
than the life of Jesus. The Father was revealed through
the Son. This is good news because it is accessible to
us through the Holy Spirit. We need the Spirit to reveal
the truth of God's character to our hearts; he brings
true understanding and revelation. God in us is an
extraordinary gift.

Let's not ignore the beauty and power of Jesus' words,
ministry, and character. The same God who laid down
his life so we could know him is the God who dwells in
heavenly places. We have been given access to the fullness
of his kingdom. What a loving God he is, and what a
humble servant too. If you want to know God, spend time
in the gospels learning more about Jesus. As you do, ask
the Holy Spirit to bring deeper revelation to your heart.

Jesus, what a beautiful Savior you are. Thank you
for making the character of God known through
your life, death, and resurrection. I look to you
today and every day.

NOT UNUSUAL

"You are blessed when they insult you and persecute you and falsely say every kind of evil against you because of me. Be glad and rejoice, because your reward is great in heaven. For that is how they persecuted the prophets who were before you."

MATTHEW 5:11-12 CSB

When we choose to follow Christ, we don't escape the troubles of this life. It doesn't mean everyone will like us. We choose to live in the overflow of his love anyway. Jesus was not violent; he healed people and gave the poor hope. The ones who hated him were religious men who thought they knew better than he did what God was like.

When we choose paths that follow Jesus' ways, we should not be surprised when some people are offended by our choices. Loving others the way Christ loved is a radical act. It will astonish some and upset others—even some who claim to know God. It's still worth it.

Jesus, your love transformed many lives, and it offended others. May I be found in you, humble and kind, rather than with those who hurl insults at others. Blessed am I when I receive the same reaction you got for choosing the ways of the kingdom.

THE RISK OF LOVE

While they were reclining at the table eating, he said,
"Truly I tell you, one of you will betray me—
one who is eating with me."
MARK 14:18 NIV

When we love others, there is no guarantee how they will treat us. We can't control whether the people we are closest to will choose to stay or leave. In Jesus' case, he knew Judas would betray him, and he still chose to give him the same love he gave his other disciples.

1 Corinthians 13 details a thorough explanation of God's love. It is patient and kind. It does not dishonor others, and it doesn't seek selfish gain. It always protects, trusts, hopes, and perseveres. This is love Jesus shows us. Will we choose to nurture and extend the same love to others? Love is always a risk, but it's one worth taking.

Lord, thank you for not putting any stipulations on your love. I receive it freely. Help me give it to others in my life without trying to protect myself in the process. I trust you.

START WITH YOURSELF

"Why do you look at the speck in your brother's eye,
but do not consider the plank in your own eye?"
MATTHEW 7:3 NKJV

It's important to slow down our assumptions when we leap to judge others. We sometimes overlook our faults in the process, so we must always begin with ourselves. We can only work on our own hearts; we can't control what anyone else does or doesn't do. We can't leap to judge, but we can always love.

There is no manipulation in the love of Christ. In light of this, we can focus on ways we can grow in love. What mindsets keep us from walking in the liberty of God's mercy? What habits stick us in cycles of fear or shame? Before we judge anyone for their choices, let's look at the choices we make as well as our hearts' motives. This is our duty.

Jesus, forgive me for moments when I jump to assumptions about others' motives while excusing my own failures. Focus me on my heart and home first so I can, with your gracious help, do the work you've given me. Thank you.

GO IN PEACE

"Daughter, your faith has made you well;
go in peace and be cured of your disease."
MARK 5:34 NASB

We all need the peace of Christ in our hearts. When we dare to believe he can heal us, we experience the generosity of his power, and he sends us forth in peace. We can always believe in God for the fulfillment we long for. He never misunderstands our motives, and his heart always responds to ours.

When we experience the power of God's mercy, there is no reason to feel guilty about our need for mercy. Our breakthrough will help others believe and ask for mercy too. Instead, let's move confidently in the peace of Christ and be free from our suffering. Shame has no foothold in a heart secure in the liberty of Christ's love.

Healer, when I dare to believe you are my great liberator, you flood me with the wonderful peace of your loving kindness. Thank you, Jesus. A thousand times, thank you! I will not stop sharing your goodness with people in my life.

FAITHFUL TEACHER

When he had washed their feet and put on his outer
garments and resumed his place, he said to them,
"Do you understand what I have done to you?"
JOHN 13:12 ESV

Jesus took the time to wash each of his disciples' feet
before they shared their last Passover meal together. It
was a humble and powerful act, yet Jesus did not just let
the action speak for itself. He wanted to make sure his
friends understood the reason behind it.

Jesus is an incredible, faithful teacher. He instructs us, but
he also takes the time to help us understand. Knowing
how patient he is, may we learn to wait on the Lord. When
we spend time in fellowship with him, we make room for
our hearts to learn from him. He is always ready to teach
us the deeper meaning of his ways if we will listen.

Messiah, thank you for the incredible patience of your
heart toward me. Teach me, Lord, for I am your willing
student.

PERFECT FULFILLMENT

"If you think I've come to set aside the law of Moses or the writings of the prophets, you're mistaken. I have come to fulfill and bring to perfection all that has been written."
MATTHEW 5:17 TPT

Jesus is the perfect fulfillment of the requirements of the law. He satisfied every prophecy, and he instructed his followers in the underlying principles of the laws of the Old Testament. Christ did not abolish the law of Moses; he brought it to perfection. His standard is now ours.

God didn't overlook a single detail in the life and ministry of Christ. Every prophetic declaration about the Messiah was fulfilled in his time on the earth. This is how we know Jesus is the Christ. He also moved in mighty, miraculous power as Son of God and Son of Man. He is the fulfillment of every longing in the heavens, on the earth, and in each of our hearts.

Messiah, thank you for fulfilling the law perfectly for us. My heart longs to be satisfied in the living love of your presence. I am glad you are alive and still moving in the earth and through your people.

KEEP WATCH

"I will come as unexpectedly as a thief! Blessed are all who are watching for me, who keep their clothing ready so they will not have to walk around naked and ashamed."
REVELATION 16:15 NLT

Time is fleeting. We don't know when Christ will return, and we don't know how many days we have before we leave this earth. Our lives are short. Do we make the most of each day? Do our loved ones know how dearly we care about them?

Let's not grow tired in living with the values of Christ's kingdom in full view. We must make sure our priorities are what we want them to be. If we live with a passion to know God and to share his love with others, we have nothing to worry about. We keep watch by watching how we live. With faith, not sight, as our guide, we set our eyes on things above and live for what truly matters.

Jesus, I know you are coming again. Instead of letting that fill me with fear, I choose to see it with excitement. It means I get to live for you now and live with hopeful expectation that you are coming to set every wrong thing right.

LEARNED BEHAVIOR

"I am telling you what my Father has shown me,
but you do what your father has told you."
JOHN 8:38 NCV

We learn by example. Think of small children. Do they not mimic what they see others doing? Aren't we surprised or delighted (depending on what it is) when they repeat what we say in off-hand moments? We come into this world as blank slates, but we don't stay that way for long.

What of those of us who are fully-grown? What must we unlearn to walk in the ways of Christ? Though we have many conditioned responses and thought patterns, with intention, time, and grace, we can shed things that don't serve us, Christ, or others, and learn Jesus' ways. It's never too late. It just starts with the humility and willingness to admit we got it wrong. There is grace and mercy to meet us, free us, and teach us.

Christ, I yield my heart to your leadership. There are things I think are right because others demonstrated or taught it to me when in reality, it is not your truth. I humble myself to learn your perfect ways.

UNCLOUDED HEARTS

"The eye is the lamp of the body. If your eye is healthy,
your whole body will be full of light."

MATTHEW 6:22 CSB

The eyes of our spirits allow the revealing light of Christ to enter us. The light floods in when our hearts are unclouded. How do we remain clear? When we keep ourselves from loving money, belongings, and success more than we love God, we keep our eyes healthy. If we try to serve both God and the opinion of others, we will fail, for they are competing interests.

Is there anything clouding your heart from receiving the full revelation of Christ? Take some time with the Lord in prayer and invite him to bring to mind what is getting in the way. Are you willing to repent and ask him to clear your heart with his mercy? There is more than enough grace for you. Lean in.

Jesus, you are the light of my life, and I don't want any competing interest getting in your way. Shine your light on my heart and reveal areas I still need to surrender to you. Thank you.

HOUSE OF PRAYER

"It is written," he said to them,
"'My house will be a house of prayer';
but you have made it 'a den of robbers.'"
LUKE 19:46 NIV

When Jesus walked into the temple and saw it bustling with merchants selling all sorts of things to vulnerable worshipers, he acted. He flipped the tables, forced out the merchants, and rebuked them. He was angry and rightly so.

The house of God is meant to be a house of prayer for all nations. In the new covenant of Christ, the people of God are the temple of God. 1 Corinthians 3:16 says, "Don't you know that you yourselves are God's temple and that God's Spirit dwells in your midst?" If we are houses of God, we should be filled with prayer too. We could fill ourselves with consumerism that continually begs for more to be satisfied. Instead, let's posture our hearts in prayer and find our satisfaction in the presence of God within us.

Jesus, I am yours. Drive out what does not belong in me as I submit my heart to you again.

INTEGRITY MATTERS

"Unless your righteousness exceeds the righteousness of the scribes and Pharisees, you will by no means enter the kingdom of heaven."

MATTHEW 5:20 NKJV

Righteousness is not empty works; it is virtue that encompasses our hearts and emanates from the inside out. Though the scribes and Pharisees knew God's Word, they did not know God. Their righteousness was only skin-deep. They knew the right things to say, and they believed they had full understanding, but it did nothing to either impress or fool Jesus.

The fruit of the Pharisees was revealed when they conspired to murder Jesus. The same is true for us. We can't hide our true motives, bitterness, or pride. Eventually, what is within will come out. This is why integrity matters. When we live authentic, humble lives submitted to Christ, his righteousness becomes ours. It covers our hearts, minds, and lives, and it transforms us.

Righteous One, thank you for the power of your mercy that offers your righteousness as my own. I can't thank you enough. I don't need to appear put-together to the world; I just want to be known as yours.

EXPANDING KINGDOM

"Nor will they say, 'Look, here it is!' or, 'There it is!'
For behold, the kingdom of God is in your midst."
LUKE 17:21 NASB

The kingdom of God can't be pinned to one place. It is a spiritual kingdom as well as a physical one. Jesus said the coming of his kingdom could not be observed by the naked eye. It is in our midst; it is within us.

Jesus Christ is the fullness of the kingdom. He brings it with him wherever he is, and his Spirit does the same. Christ is alive in us by faith, and so is the reality of his kingdom. Like his limitless love, it is ever-expanding. If we live as those who have the kingdom of Christ always available, where there is abundance of grace, peace, joy, and love, we have courage to face whatever comes our way. We are never alone.

Jesus Christ, your kingdom is my home, and it is closer than my skin. Thank you for the reality of your presence that rules and reigns within me. Expand my understanding of your glory as I praise you.

DIVINE ENCOURAGER

"I tell you the truth: it is to your advantage that I go away,
for if I do not go away, the Helper will not come to you.
But if I go, I will send him to you."

JOHN 16:7 ESV

When Jesus was on earth, he was bound by a human body. He could not be in every place at once. He submitted to the experience of being fully human, so he was also under the laws of nature as we know them. Jesus knew once he left, the Holy Spirit would come and empower every person who submits to him.

The Spirit is not something to fear. The Spirit is our greatest gift. Like wind, we cannot see him, but we can feel his effects. When the Spirit blows, we feel the breath of his presence. We feel the refreshment of his tangible love. We experience the comfort he brings to our grief, needed encouragement when we are downhearted, and the power required to persist when we are completely depleted of strength.

Jesus, thank you for sending your Spirit. He is a wonderful comforter, teacher, and helper. Thank you for all I get to experience through you.

LOVE YOUR ENEMY

"Love your enemies and do something wonderful
for them in return for their hatred."
LUKE 6:27 TPT

It is not enough to tolerate those we don't like. Jesus tells us we should love our enemies. How? By doing something wonderful for them. We don't return their curses with more curses; we give them blessings instead.

This is not something we can do in our own strength. We must find our identity firmly rooted in the eyes of God and not in the opinions of others. If we care too much about what others think of us, when we make enemies, we will avoid them. Instead, we are called to love them, bless them, and always choose the higher path.

Jesus, I look to your example for how to love my enemies. Your enemies deeply hated you; they murdered you. And yet, you loved them fully. Help me be more like you especially when it's difficult.

HIGHER STANDARDS

"If you are even angry with someone, you are subject to judgment! If you call someone an idiot, you are in danger of being brought before the court. And if you curse someone, you are in danger of the fires of hell."

MATTHEW 5:22 NLT

Jesus leveled the playing field for all people. Never murdered anyone? Well, if you've been angry with someone, you're no better off. Never had an affair? If you've lusted after someone, you basically did the same thing. Jesus was making a point; we are all sinners. We all fall short of the glory of God.

That's why we need Jesus. We need his mercy. If we think too highly of ourselves, we fool ourselves into thinking we're above reproach, but none of us are. Pride goes before a fall for a reason. May we not look at today's verse and feel shame. Rather, we can feel the relief that was meant. We can't perfectly keep the requirements of the law. Jesus came so we could be made right in his own righteousness, and we all have equal access to this gift.

Savior, I love that no one has a right to you more another. Class, job, identity, nationality, and education don't matter. You offer the same perfect righteousness to all who come to the Father through you. Thank you.

BLESS YOUR ENEMIES

"Bless those who curse you,
pray for those who are cruel to you."
LUKE 6:28 NCV

When we bless those who curse us and pray for those who are cruel to us, we soften our hearts in the process. When we can do this, we keep our hearts pliant in the loving kindness of Jesus.

He did this first. He does not ask us to do what he wouldn't do himself. Jesus did not condemn his murderers. He prayed that the Father would forgive them. He extended mercy to every person who hated him. When we align ourselves with Christ, we have his grace to empower us to follow him. There is blessing, not only for others, but blessing that returns to us when we pray for those who are cruel to him.

Jesus, I choose to do what you taught when you said to love your enemy and bless those who curse you. I lay down my right to vengeance and bitterness. I know you always have our best at heart, and your ways are full of wisdom. I need your help to do this.

CAN'T MISS HIM

> "Then if anyone tells you,
> 'See, here is the Messiah!
> See, there!' do not believe it."
> MARK 13:21 CSB

We can't be fooled about Jesus' return. He told his disciples it would be obvious, so we need not fear that we could miss him. A few verses later, Jesus described what it will be like: "They will see 'the Son of Man coming in the clouds' with great power and glory" (vs. 26). The idea that anyone could miss such a sight is out of the question.

Many things in the world threaten our faith, but our roots can grow so deeply in the truth of Christ that we cannot be fooled. God's wisdom grounds us in peace. We don't have to scare people (including ourselves) into belief. Perfect love casts out fear. Let's rest in the knowledge that Christ will come in the clouds for everyone to see. He will not hide himself.

Messiah, I don't have to live under fear any longer. Your love has overcome every fear, and I get to live in the liberty of your truth. What joy and peace are mine! Thank you.

MERCY AND COMPASSION

"Be merciful,
just as your Father is merciful."
LUKE 6:36 NIV

God the Father overflows with mercy and compassion for all. This isn't wishful thinking; it's the truth Jesus came to reveal to our hearts! Just as our heavenly Father bursts with this kind of love, may we offer the same compassion and mercy to others.

When we choose to do this, we give out of what has been poured into us. We reflect lessons learned under God's guidance. When we are merciful as God is merciful, we do not hold grudges, we allow for the mistakes of others, and we leave room for people to change their minds. These are just a few examples. Take some time to think about other practical ways to display mercy in your life.

Merciful One, thank you for showing us what the Father is truly like. I submit to your teaching, and I will look to you until I begin to reflect your nature in my life. May I be clothed in your compassion and mercy and give it freely to others.

WALK IN THE LIGHT

"Are there not twelve hours in the day? If anyone walks in the day, he does not stumble, because he sees the light of this world. But if one walks in the night, he stumbles, because the light is not in him."

JOHN 11:9-10 NKJV

It's much easier to travel in the light of the day than in the dark of night. What we miss in the darkness, we see easily with the sun shining down on us. Jesus is like the sun. He lights our days with the radiance of his glory. His truth is a lamp to our feet and a light to our path.

Have you been trying to forge a path alone? Why not ask the Lord for guidance? When he shines his light, you may realize the path is riddled with obstacles you had not seen. You may choose to redirect your path in light of what he reveals. Whatever you do, trust him to guide you. Look to him for leadership and walk in the light he gives.

Radiant One, you are the light that shines in the darkness. I don't want to force my way through darkness, stumbling and questioning, when I could wait for your perspective and walk with confidence. Shine on me, Lord.

IT STILL MATTERS

"Until heaven and earth pass away,
not the smallest letter or stroke of a letter
shall pass from the Law, until all is accomplished!"
MATTHEW 5:18 NASB

As we wait on the Lord's return, there are still prophecies that must come to pass. There are things written in Scripture that have not yet happened. Jesus did not nullify these things. He said that everything written would be fulfilled. Until the end of this age, there is still power and purpose in the Bible.

Though our understanding of Scripture may change, the power of Scripture does not. The Word of God is full of stories of faithful ones who, though far from perfect, were used by God. There are Scriptures to encourage, strengthen, and help us. Some verses give wisdom to very natural problems; others offer us hope. The Word of God is living and active, and it never returns void.

Jesus, your Word is a wonderful gift to all who believe. Through it, we find your character clearly revealed. May I find what I need in your Word today.

GIVE GENEROUSLY

"Give, and it will be given to you. Good measure,
pressed down, shaken together, running over,
will be put into your lap. For with the measure
you use it will be measured back to you."

LUKE 6:38 ESV

One of the greatest principles of Christ's kingdom is
generosity. The more you give, the more you receive.
Interesting, isn't it? When we focus on retaining what
we have, we lose the privilege and power of generosity.
However, we can change course at any moment. Will we
hoard our resources, or will we try to outdo one another in
lavish and practical giving?

Whatever measure of giving we choose will be used for
our returning gift. Shouldn't that knowledge increase our
benevolence? If we want to make room for greater things,
we must be willing to make a change. Hesitancy will keep
us stuck in same patterns. If we want to receive more, we
must be willing to make room for it by giving what we
already have.

Generous Jesus, there is no one more giving than you.
You gave your very life so we could know you. I loosen
my grip and ask for your grace as I begin expanding my
generosity with intention.

I AM

"I give you this eternal truth:
I have existed long before Abraham was born,
for I AM!"
JOHN 8:58 TPT

Long before Abraham, Christ was present with his Father. Father, Spirit, and Son were together from the beginning. The first coming of Christ was extremely natural. He was born to a young woman and her new husband. Jesus was born among stable animals as there was no private room available. How is it that the God beyond time, the great I AM, degraded himself to be born in such a humble way?

The life Jesus led was not glamorous. In his ministry days, he didn't even have a home to return to at night. He traveled around, not taking much with him, but he had all he needed. No matter how little we have to offer Jesus today, it doesn't matter. Let's wholeheartedly offer it knowing he loves simple and humble things.

I Am, thank you for coming as a humble baby and for subjecting yourself to the human experience. I am not ashamed to offer you what is mine. I love you, Jesus.

NARROW GATE

"You can enter God's Kingdom only through the narrow gate. The highway to hell is broad, and its gate is wide for the many who choose that way."

MATTHEW 7:13 NLT

Why is gate of God's kingdom narrow? Is it because it is hard to find, or rather because so few choose it that it remains small? Although the gospel of Christ is incredibly simple, that does not mean that it's easy to choose. The way of love is always the less popular route.

With loud voices telling us that bigger is better, destruction is normal, and greed is okay, it can be hard to tune in to the still, small voice that beckons us to follow a different path. When we choose to submit to Christ's ways, we lay down our rights. Are we willing to transform our thinking, our way of life, and our approach to others? With love as our guide, we will find the narrow gate.

Jesus, I want to walk in the power of your love, and I know this means I must lay down my offense at what I think is right. No matter how hard it is, I want to choose love at every turn. Lead me, and I will follow.

TRUE OVERFLOW

"Good people bring good things out of the good they stored in their hearts. But evil people bring evil things out of the evil they stored in their hearts. People speak the things that are in their hearts."

LUKE 6:45 NCV

People are known by the fruit of their lives. With this in mind, what do you think your life says to others? Look past your successes and failures and more closely at the relationships you have built, the meals you have shared, and the impact your generosity has had. Your life is built by the choices you make, the heart behind them, and the follow-through.

If you don't like the fruit of your life, look inward. What is your heart focused on? What motivations drive your actions? If God can change hearts of stone into hearts of flesh, Jesus can transform yours if you let him.

Jesus, transform my heart in the power of your mercy. I want to reflect your nature in my life. May your nurturing bring an abundance of good fruit in my heart.

ALL IS FORGIVEN

Just then some men brought to him a paralytic lying
on a stretcher. Seeing their faith, Jesus told the paralytic,
"Have courage, son, your sins are forgiven."
MATTHEW 9:2 CSB

Jesus knows exactly what we need to hear just when we
need to hear it. When Jesus told the paralytic man his sins
were forgiven, it must have been a relief to that man's
heart. Perhaps he wondered what he had done to deserve
his injury. Maybe he had wrestled over sin that kept him in
shame. Whatever the case, Jesus offered what no one else
could: true and lasting forgiveness for the man's sins.

Is there a sin you just haven't been able to shake the
effects of? Has shame kept you laid out and too paralyzed
to move on? May you receive the words of Christ today in
your heart and life as he says to you, "Take heart; your sins
are forgiven."

Lord Jesus, thank you for your freeing forgiveness. I feel
the relief your mercy brings. I praise you!

REACH OUT

"Can the blind lead the blind?
Will they not both fall into a pit?"
LUKE 6:39 NIV

It is one thing for a blind person to rely on another person to help them along; it is entirely another for a blind person to guide another blind person. This comparison applies to our spiritual journey too. If we know we don't see perfectly, we should not rely on someone else whose vision is equally impaired to guide us.

Where does this leave us? Perhaps instead of relying on advice and opinions from people who have no idea, let's rely on the leadership of Christ who sees all, knows all, and can help us avoid the pitfalls of life. He is our ultimate example, for there is nothing he did not overcome. What he overcame, he can help us through. Reach out and take his hand today.

Jesus, it seems everyone has strong opinions about everything, but yours is the truth I follow. I trust you to guide me in the nuances of this life. Your perspective means more to me than any other.

TRUE FINDINGS

"Even if I do judge, My judgment is true;
for I am not alone in it, but I and the Father who sent Me."
JOHN 8:16 NASB

When Jesus said we should not judge unless we want to be judged, the standard applied to him too. As he clearly stated, Jesus did not come to condemn the world but to save the world. Even so, if Jesus had chosen to judge, it would have been true because Jesus, as God, has perfect judgment.

For those of us who believe and follow him, the principle has not shifted. If we judge others, which we know we can't do rightly because we don't know the heart of a person, we will be judged in the same way. Let's leave the judgment with God and move in mercy just as Jesus taught us.

Jesus Christ, I trust you to judge what needs to be judged, and I choose to walk in your mercy. I leave behind my assumptions; instead, I will leave room for people to surprise me. Thank you for your help in this.

PUT INTO PRACTICE

"What good does it do for you to say I am your Lord and
Master if what I teach you is not put into practice?"
Luke 6:46 TPT

As you look ahead to the new year and the fresh start it
brings, may you go into it with Christ as your loving leader.
He has given you everything you need, and his teaching
contains all you need to know to move forward. You don't
have to see the full picture yet; simply take the next steps
you know are yours to take.

The more you grow, the more he will reveal, and the more
he reveals, the more you will have to put into practice.
Trust the leadership of Christ not only with your mind and
heart but with your very life. There is room to practice
and get it wrong. He doesn't expect perfection. He knows
you through and through already. You'll never grow if you
don't start, so use this opportunity of a new calendar year
to start, however small, by practicing what you preach.

Lord, thank you for the practicality of your teachings.
I won't just say I believe them; I will put them into
practice with your grace and help. Thank you for being a
patient teacher. I love you!